D1009783

Overcoming Underachieving

Other Books by Ruth Peters

Who's in Charge?

Don't Be Afraid to Discipline

It's Never Too Soon to Discipline

Overcoming Underachieving

A Simple Plan to
Boost Your Kids' Grades and
End the Homework Hassles

Dr. Ruth Peters

Broadway Books   New York

BROADWAY

OVERCOMING UNDERACHIEVING. Copyright © 2000 by Dr. Ruth Peters.
All rights reserved. Printed in the United States of America. No part of this book
may be reproduced or transmitted in any form or by any means, electronic or
mechanical, including photocopying, recording, or by any information storage
and retrieval system, without written permission from the publisher. For
information, address Broadway Books, a division of Random House, Inc.,
1540 Broadway, New York, NY 10036.

Broadway Books titles may be purchased for business or promotional use or for
special sales. For information, please write to: Special Markets Department,
Random House, Inc., 1540 Broadway, New York, NY 10036.

BROADWAY BOOKS and its logo, a letter B bisected on the diagonal, are trademarks
of Broadway Books, a division of Random House, Inc.

Visit our website at www.broadwaybooks.com

Library of Congress Cataloging-in-Publication Data
Peters, Ruth Allen.
Overcoming underachieving: a simple plan to boost your kids'
grades and end the homework hassles / Ruth Peters.—1st ed.
p. cm.
1. Motivation in education. 2. Education—Parent participation.
3. Study skills. I. Title.
LB1065.P464 2000
371.3'028'1—dc21   00-024990

FIRST EDITION

Designed by Ellen Cipriano

ISBN 0-7679-0458-3

00 01 02 03 04 10 9 8 7 6 5 4 3 2 1

To Tim, Lindsay,
and Chris—with my love,
always

Confidentiality Note

~~~~~~~

Names and identifying details in the case histories reported within this book have been changed. All reported cases are real, and permission to report them has been given by the parent or guardian.

Acknowledgments

~~~~~~

Thanks to the kids and their parents who have learned from as well as taught me about human nature and what makes people tick!

With heartfelt appreciation to Jean Loveland, transcriptionist extraordinaire, whose help with this manuscript was priceless.

A very special thank you to my literary agent, Jan Miller, who never fails to come through, and my editors at Broadway Books: Suzanne Oaks for believing in the project right from the get-go, and Bob Asahina for his continued loyalty and support.

And, as always, hugs and kisses to Tim and the kids for sharing their summer with this project!

Contents

~~~~~

Perhaps the most valuable result of
all education is the ability to make yourself do
the thing you have to do when it
ought to be done whether you like it or not.

—THOMAS HENRY HUXLEY

Introduction

~~~~~

As a clinical psychologist working with children and adolescents for over two decades, sometimes I think I've seen just about everything—skinny kids who want to be heavier, fat kids who dream of being stick-thin, shy children who rarely utter a word, and extroverts who can't seem to keep a thought to themselves. Little kids, grade-schoolers, teenagers—you name it, I've seen a bunch of them.

And then there's the parents, those who are too domineering and protective juxtaposed with believers in a laissez-faire, let 'em sink-or-swim philosophy of child rearing. Parents who are afraid to discipline and those who are just itching to grab a switch. Young parents (still kids themselves), thirtysomethings, middle-agers, as well as grandparents who are starting over raising their grandkids as their own.

I've seen lots of problems as well as solutions, pain as well as joy. And I've come to realize that we're all in this together. Raising kids truly is a community effort with influences from teachers, preachers, pediatricians, in-laws, as well as peers.

As a parent myself, I've experienced indecision and regret, weakness and strength. I have reveled in my own kids' achievements and marveled at their talents, as well as becoming frustrated during moments of stubbornness or rebellion. I've come to the conclusion, both as a mom and a psychologist, that we're all in the same boat—searching for ways to promote our children to achieve as well as to become self-sufficient.

Over the years, though, I've witnessed a disturbing trend in the types of kids coming to my office for help. Not only do they seem to be more rebellious than their predecessors a decade ago, but their academic motivation and willingness to do whatever it takes to succeed in school seems to be declining. These children lack organizational skills, are not particularly interested in managing their time appropriately, and seem not to care about the grades that they receive. Their folks, on the other hand, are becoming increasingly concerned, generally reacting by nagging, hand-wringing, grounding, or just plain giving up.

As a result of this trend toward underachievement and the resulting family problems, I've developed a program for my clients consisting of study skills and organizational techniques that I teach to the kids, as well as behavior management guidelines for their parents to use to motivate their children. I've found that both parts are necessary for kids to achieve good grades—your son can learn brilliant organizational skills, but unless he's motivated to use them on a consistent basis, he probably won't. Plain and simple.

And that's how and why I've come to specialize in the area of motivating underachieving students. Seeing good minds wasted due to procrastination, disorganization, or laziness is just not acceptable and we, as parents, must be the ones to step in and guide our kids. My efforts take the form not only of this book, but also of years of lecturing throughout the country to parents, educators, and mental health workers about jump-starting their kids' academic efforts. I've served as the Study Skills Consultant to Sylvan Learning Systems nationwide and I have written magazine articles and numerous newspaper columns on this subject. I've also taken my passion to national television, discussing this issue on shows ranging from *Oprah* to *Montel Williams* and serving as a contributor to *Good Morning America* and *Later Today*.

And I believe that my efforts are paying off. Not only to do the kids in my private practice sport better grades, but I receive gratifying letters from folks who've used my system and are not only grateful for the better grades, but also for the family harmony that results.

In this book I give to you my study skills program for use with your own family. I will teach you how to take charge and to motivate your kids to develop the skills and self-control necessary to succeed in today's academic environment. Through the following chapters you'll be introduced to the six types of underachieving kids that I most often see in my practice. Your child will either fit neatly into one category or may display a blend of behaviors of two or even three types. A short quiz will help you to decide what type of underachiever your child is and the kinds of behaviors you can expect.

As well as identifying the style of your student, you'll be introduced to the six most common mistakes parents make in dealing with their academically frustrating kids. Are you a *leave-it-to-the-teacher* type of parent, depending solely upon the school to motivate your child? Or do you believe in *peace-at-any-price*, crossing your fingers and hoping the kid does his homework and stays on top of things without any fuss from you? A quiz will help you to gain insight into which parenting mistakes you're making and you'll see how both you and your child have fallen into ineffective study patterns.

Once you've reviewed the various types of underachieving kids and the mistakes that parents typically make, I'll present the parenting style that works best for all kids— that of the *benevolent dictator*. This type of parenting is not only fair, but it gets the results that you want—kids actively participating in making appropriate goals and fulfilling their responsibilities. (By the way, this parenting style is also great for getting children to make their beds and to take out the dog!)

Next we'll review some basic behavioral techniques for effective parenting that work *with* kid human nature not *against* it. I'll describe the general rules by developmental age level for ensuring your child's compliance with my study skills program, which is presented in Chapter Six. This academic achievement program really works—it's simple yet comprehensive and has helped thousands of kids and their families get on the right track, improving school grades as well as academic attitudes. Commit to following through with the program's consequences on a daily basis and you'll be amazed at the progress made in just a few weeks! Several of my own clients offer their personal experiences and you'll be inspired by their testimonials. These are real kids from families just like yours who have turned their academic lives around by following my study skills program.

We'll also review special situations leading to academic underachievement and how to use my study skills program with kids who've missed some early academic fundamentals, or display the symptoms of Attention Deficit Disorder, or have been diagnosed with a learning difference.

What you'll learn from this book is exactly what I present to families in therapy at my office. Just as they've succeeded in motivating their children to achieve not only good grades, but *great grades*, you too can be successful in motivating your child to achieve in school. Whether this information is given in a therapy session or read in this book, it's just as valid, effective, and capable of changing your child's life. Together we can work through this process and motivate your child to work to his full potential!

one

But Madison's Mom Doesn't Even Check Her Report Card!

~~~~~~~

Try this one on for size—you know your twelve-year-old is smart—he can beat just about any video game he puts his mind to and can successfully work a crowd, displaying social skills that would have impressed even Dale Carnegie. When in a pinch (perhaps the night before an assignment is due), he can produce a short essay relating the effect of the deterioration of the ozone layer upon photosynthesis that not only makes sense, but makes you wonder where he got his smarts from. You know he can do it—but does so only when he's pushed, or there's something in it for him, or he's just plain enthralled with the subject matter.

So why is this kid just squeaking by in school? His report card reflects good grades in the few classes he enjoys, yet yield D's and even F's in those he perceives as boring or useless. If he's like most of my underachieving clients, the answers lie in those microscopic letters ("comment codes") placed next to the academic grades on middle or high school report cards or in the columns devoted to study habits and behavior on grade school report cards. To make my point, I've pulled out my sixteen-year-old's latest one. The available comment codes are as follows:

1. Class Preparation Is Poor

2. Test Scores Are Low

3. Student Does Not Complete Required Assignments

4. Student Does Not Bring Materials to Class

5. Student Displays Poor Attitude

6. Behavior Is Poor

Grade school report cards provide similar information, but these areas are generally labeled as E for excellent, S for satisfactory, I for improvement needed, or U for unsatisfactory.

Children who receive negative comment codes are usually those who evidence poor preparation, disorganization, laziness, or a general lack of motivation regarding school. Class grades of D's and F's are followed by a smattering of 1's, 2's, and 3's or I's and U's, whereas kids who earn good grades usually receive few negative comment codes. The pattern is clear—when kids display good study skills and habits (paying attention in class, completing class work and homework, studying for tests, and turning in requirements on time) they earn good grades. Equally as predictable are D's and F's followed by comment codes for poor preparation, not bringing materials to class, or inappropriate behavior, all of which indicate inadequate study skills resulting in little learning.

What's Gravity Got to Do with It?

Just like the apple hitting the ground after it falls from the tree, Johnny's grades head south as his study skills plummet. The concept of gravity is a law of *physical nature*, the connection between study habits and academic achievement is a law of *human nature*. As a child/adolescent psychologist, my job is to work with human nature—to reason, argue, convince, and to even manipulate kids into doing what's best for them. Many kids see little value in what I or their folks are suggesting and feel that our goals are either nonsensical, unimportant, or just plain inconvenient.

That's okay—viewing adult "sense" as "nonsense" is the stuff of childhood and adolescence. It would be nice if kids perceived life's priorities as adults do, but most just don't. Kids base their perceptions of value on their small amount of life experience, many tend to be impulsive and to live for the moment, and a major priority is having fun. That's normal kid human nature, you might as well accept it. There are some children with more mature views (generally teased as dorks or nerds by classmates, admired by teachers, and taken credit for by parents), but these tend to be exceptions to the rule. Self-motivated kids who put schoolwork before Nintendo, read because the book is fascinating, and take pride in their homework are well outnumbered by the masses of unmotivated children. Most of us do not own such a child. We may know of one or have heard stories about the driven kid down the block, but most of us are not fortunate enough to have one living under our own roof!

Parents, on the other hand, have developed some amount of wisdom gained from years of both successes and failures. Most of us have finally figured out that playing by the rules is more productive than ignoring them and that persistence and hard work usually pay off. More important, though, is the realization that forcing ourselves to do things that we either don't want to do, are bored with, or are even totally disinterested in is part of the self-discipline needed to succeed in our jobs, our marriages, and especially in raising our own children.

Sure, we still like to have a good time, but we've assigned fun to a somewhat lower position on our scale of priorities. It's hard to be in a playful mood if you've just been fired from your job for repeatedly coming to work late or failing to complete the projects that are assigned to you. Spouses get annoyed when promises are not kept and kids tend to become bratty when their folks don't have the self-discipline themselves to follow through with the consequences threatened. We've learned to put work before play and most of us have been rewarded for doing so. We're now less impulsive than as teens and put fun in its rightful place—as a *necessary* ingredient of a fulfilled life, but not as the *main* ingredient. Also, many have realized that a good performance is highly rewarding in and of itself, be it perfecting a computer program, helping a client in distress, or surprising one's spouse by taking out the trash just because it needs to be done!

Sadly, though, there are adults who have not yet become self-motivated and self-disciplined. Due to a variety of reasons, they have been able, allowed, or even encouraged to grow up without having developed adequate frustration tolerance. These folks tend to drop out of school (even though they may have been described as brilliant at an earlier age), have difficulty keeping jobs (due to not being able to stay motivated or focused when the work becomes too boring or too challenging), and generally have a rough time maintaining a marriage (when the going gets tough, they're out of there).

What do adult job failures and marital problems have in common with kid academic underachievement? Just about everything because all of these behaviors are symptoms of the same underlying problem—a distinct lack of self-discipline and poor frustration tolerance. Kids generally are not internally motivated to achieve in school or to do homework. Math problems can be tedious, boring, and have no discernible value if you plan to play first base for a living. This is typical kid logic, whether in kindergarten or eleventh grade, the value of education escapes them. *That's okay*—it's the nature of the beast. *It's not okay,* though, for kids to become adults who behave in this manner. The real world will not tolerate a slacker and employers have little patience for tardiness or for fooling around on the job.

Marianne is such an individual. At twenty-eight years

old, she's already had thirteen jobs ranging from telemarketer to nurse's aide. I'd been seeing her younger brother due to issues surrounding their parents' recent separation and her mom had described how Marianne was again living at home, disgruntled at being dependent upon her mother, but not having the funds to move out on her own. Apparently this was a pattern with Marianne—she would have great expectations (earlier in high school declaring that she would be valedictorian) when taking on a new job (vowing to wow her boss with the sales she'd produce) or entering into a relationship (certain that this would be the big one). Yet time and again Marianne's initial fervor would decline and when the work became boring she would begin to put it off, resulting in a low high school GPA and getting fired for lack of sustained effort or coming in late to work. Her latest relationship had fizzled when her boyfriend refused to continue paying the rent tab as Marianne seemed to constantly be in need of funds.

Her mother reported that Marianne had always lacked perseverance, tended to give up easily, and was allowed to quit because she and her husband just didn't have the emotional energy to force the issues as they cropped up. They hoped that Marianne would grow up, see the light, and begin to use self-discipline.

Well, apparently self-discipline had yet to kick in, as their daughter was back home again, mooching off of her mom. It's difficult to use self-discipline when you've never really learned it in the first place. Had her parents had the stamina to insist upon acquiring frustration tolerance skills back in middle and high school by expecting good grades and not accepting mediocre ones, Marianne most likely would have developed the ability to later deal successfully with job and relationship challenges also. She would have become a self-sufficient provider, rather than a dependent taker.

The Chicken or the Egg?

One of our main roles as parents is to teach our children how to develop motivated academic *behavior* (good study habits), if not a motivated academic *attitude* (the love of learning). Some folks feel uncomfortable with this statement, that it's okay to accept appropriate behavior even if the attitude is not yet up to snuff. As a behavioral psychologist for over twenty years, I continue to believe that a child's *behavior* is what is of primary importance. Of course I'll take a good attitude—that's great—but I won't do a meltdown if the kid doesn't really *want* to complete his work, but finishes it mainly because he's *externally motivated* to do so.

Other psychologists feel that it's necessary to have a good attitude before an acceptable behavior or performance can occur, that one must be "talked into" becoming internally motivated before being able to produce a good work product. I'm sure that's true in some cases, but with many of the kids that I've seen most will become adults before the "light" truly goes on and the attitude is changed. I choose not to wait that long to establish self-disciplined behavior in my clients—I want the good grades *now*. And generally kids who are externally motivated to perform in school not only get good grades, but begin to feel confident, have higher expectations of themselves, and go on to develop a sincere achieving attitude. That's why I feel comfortable using consequences such as rewards and punishments to motivate kids to learn and use good study habits and skills. Whether this is bribing a child to do what he should be doing naturally is not the issue—many kids need motivators to begin new habits. In this sense the end does justify the means. I'll take a kid who makes good grades because he wants to earn a reward (or to avoid a punishment) over a child who's left to his own devices and chooses to accept poor grades. There's nothing wrong with short-term bribery (consequences) if it leads to true behavioral and attitudinal change (good study habits) in the long run.

It's a cycle—good study behaviors net good grades, preparedness for class, and good class participation. When kids are actively involved (asking and answering questions), the school day seems to go by faster, is definitely more interesting, and homework is quickly and easily accomplished. Parents no longer have to check up on and nag their kids to complete tasks and the home atmosphere changes from the daily drama of whether Megan will complete her math problems without throwing a fit to perhaps some family time available for playing board games or watching a video together. When your child learns good study skills and develops appropriate study habits, the bases for adult self-control and frustration tolerance are being set. It's only a small leap from getting to school on time and completing classwork to arriving promptly at work each day and completing the demands of one's position.

Even "extras," such as taking the time to attend an SAT

preparatory program, are affected by good study habits. Kids who have learned to value the outcome of an education also tend to do well on standardized tests that net admission and perhaps a scholarship to college. These kids are not only willing to take the time to prepare for the SAT, but also value the information and test-taking strategies they've learned. So teaching your kids self-discipline and good study habits will not only have a positive effect on the daily drudgery of attending school, completing work, and developing a good academic attitude, but it lightens the home atmosphere as well as helping children to maintain the motivation necessary to push forward toward college goals or their chosen vocations.

Is There a Motivational Gene?

Almost every day in my clinical practice I listen to parents grumping about their childrens' lack of motivation in school, poor report cards, and general malaise when it comes to studying, completing homework, and behaving well in school. Not only does this drive their folks nuts, it also takes its toll on the kids. Children who are not *internally motivated* to solve math problems tend to be grounded often, are constantly nagged to start, complete, and turn in their homework, and feel that their folks don't trust them. They are given fewer privileges, have poor self-concepts, and tend to be more depressed than their academically achieving counterparts. In short—both kids and their folks are miserable and that's when they show up at my office.

The bases of academic underachievement, poor study

skills, and lack of internal motivation, generally evolve into a battleground scenario. Both sides draw firm lines in the sand, often refusing to compromise or not even knowing how to make the changes necessary to lower the tension and to work on productive solutions. And it's not just in my office that the sides wage war. Throughout America our culture is feeling the shock wave of kids' academic under-achievement and lack of self-discipline. Dropout rates are at an all-time high, substance use and abuse is again on the rise following a brief respite in the late eighties, violent crimes committed by adolescents are skyrocketing as are teenage pregnancy rates. What do these behaviors have to do with Junior completing his homework?

A lot. Kids who do well in school tend to have developed personality and behavioral traits consisting of perseverance, self-control, and a stable work ethic. They usually do not possess even one IQ point higher than do their peers who perform poorly. However, they set goals, can tolerate frustration, have been taught to use study skills techniques, and understand the connection between their behaviors and the consequences they receive. That's it in a nutshell. Nothing mysterious, expensive, or unobtainable—kids who take academics seriously also tend to get into less trouble, to think before acting, and to reap the rewards of success. How do these children develop such wonderful internalized desires and goals? Are they fortunate enough to have been born with a "motivational gene" not possessed by others? I don't think so. What their parents have given them, though, is the gift of internalized motivation, often the result of their folks using external motivators to jump-start the process.

Kids wore the dunce cap in Grandma and Grandpa's day and some will continue to do so in this new century. Although no longer ostracized or physically placed in the corner of the classroom, today's underachiever faces ridicule by his peers, disappointment from his folks, and most important—the risk of developing a poor self-concept due to uncertainties about his abilities. And the consequences of academic failure are much greater today than ever before, as technology has little patience for the underskilled or unmotivated. Our children must not only be taught the three R's, but also a fourth—*responsibility*—based upon self-discipline and frustration tolerance and eventually internal motivation. Parents bear the burden, as well as the honor, of becoming their child's first and best teacher of behaviors, values, and ethics.

two

The Six Types of
Underachieving Students

~~~~~

Over the years I've worked with hundreds of families who have come to my office seeking pointers on how to help their children become better students. Parents bring them in as early as kindergarten and as late as college. These are single-parent families and stepfamilies, as well as the two-parent nuclear family. Some kids sport superior IQs whereas most have average intellectual ability and some are even below average. The families differ in many ways, yet all have children who are not working to their potential in some fashion. Their children's individual academic styles may differ, but often fall within one of several types of underachieving behavior patterns. The bottom line is that all of these folks need help. Most of the parents spend evenings arguing with and nagging their kids to perform, and their children are miserable. Although the specific complaints may differ, the solution is the same—teaching study skills so that the kids develop good study habits and responsible behaviors.

1. The If-Then Student

Probably the most common type of underachieving child is that of the *if-then student*. Let's take a look at a client of mine who could be the poster child for this category. Candice's folks were stymied—their nine-year-old daughter just couldn't seem to get her act together in school. In kindergarten through second grade her teachers had nothing but praise for the child. She was able to sit at her desk appropriately, play well with her girlfriends at recess, and was generally a well-behaved, cute kid. If the classwork interested her, she usually completed it on time, but she would dawdle on some of the tasks that were either too challenging or tedious. The latter was rare, though, until third grade when her parents began to notice more classwork papers coming home incomplete. They spoke with Candice about the problem and she explained that math was becoming difficult and that writing vocabulary sentences was just too boring.

With third grade somehow completed and now in the beginning of fourth, Candice's folks expected problems but nothing like her teacher had described to them in their most recent conference. Not only was she dawdling with her classwork, but at times Candice would not even attempt to begin it. She preferred to read her latest mystery novel or to stare out the window. What work she did begin in class was rarely completed, even as homework later that evening. The teacher was so frustrated that she referred the family to my office for help.

When I met Candice, she truly was adorable—the kind of kid whose mere presence lights up the room. I knew then that it was going to be difficult to be consistent with consequences for this kid, she was just too cute! However, she did admit to the list of crimes noted by her parents—letting classwork go, not bringing home the materials necessary to complete her homework, and at times purposefully leaving her assignment pad at school. At least Candice was honest about her poor study habits—she didn't even claim to have forgotten to bring her books home, admitting that she just didn't want to be bothered by having to do the work.

From her point of view, afternoons were for having fun—playing with the kids in the neighborhood, watching television, or reading the latest in a series of novels. She'd had enough of school at school and just didn't see the point in bringing it home with her! Candice had succeeded in the early grades because she was well-mannered and compliant, and the amount of homework had been negligible. However, her fourth grade teacher was trying to prepare her students for the rigors of middle school, having to juggle six classes (and six teachers) each day and to stay organized.

When I spoke with Candice about learning organization and study skills now, in the fourth grade, in order to be better prepared for middle school, she gave me that winning smile, giggled, and basically said that she'd worry about it later. Today was today and why would she want to deal with tomorrow now?

Her mother and father, having previously wrestled with this same conversation with Candice, rolled their eyes and gave me one of those tired parent looks. Their frustration was mounting, as they had done lots of talking to Candice, but she'd done very little listening or changing. I explained to them that their mistake had been trying to *reason with the unreasonable.* Candice was a good kid, but she couldn't yet see beyond the tip of her nose. These were intelligent parents, but they couldn't seem to get beyond the notion that since *they* saw the importance of good study habits that Candice should automatically do so also.

I confronted them with a disturbing yet very common reality—that this kid just didn't get it yet. The lightbulb hadn't come on and the wake-up call was still going unanswered. All of their whining, hand-wringing, nagging, and lecturing had been for nothing and would continue to be. Candice was an *if-then student* and they needed to change tactics with their daughter in order to get her on the right academic path.

If-then students seem to live by the motto of "If there's something important in it for me, then I'll do it. If not, then I'll probably just put it off." The *if* can be any behavior, such as bringing home a completed assignment pad or completion of homework. The *then* is the consequence— ranging from the reward of going out to play or the avoidance of a negative occurrence, such as losing television time or having to go to bed early.

As we were talking, Candice was listening and nodding her head in agreement, noting that Mom and Dad's nagging and lecturing had not been effective. When I asked her what else her parents had tried, she said that at times she wouldn't be allowed to watch television if her homework wasn't completed, but then she would just curl up on her bed with a good book. As she loved to read, losing television privileges was really not a punishment after all. I asked her what would happen if her books were taken away until her homework was done and all other fun activities were curtailed. Now that got her attention! She couldn't believe that I would suggest taking away reading—after all, weren't parents supposed to be supportive of that activity? I explained to Candice that we would be willing to take away anything if it motivated her to stay on top of her school responsibilities.

We had hit a nerve—found something that Candice enjoyed enough (reading) that would motivate her to do something that she didn't like to do (classwork and homework). Her folks had been on the wrong track, having used consequences that really didn't matter to her. Kids like Candice are politely noncompliant—they still don't do what they're supposed to, even though they are well-mannered about it. The trick is to find external reinforcers (the *then*) that will motivate them to complete the desired task (the *if*).

It's not unusual for parents to feel somewhat uncomfortable with this concept. I'm often asked if this is the equivalent of bribing kids to do their work. The answer is yes, it is bribery, but so are the following scenarios:

- No dessert until you've attempted to eat dinner.

- No allowance unless your behavior last week was appropriate.

- No driver's license unless you've proven yourself to be responsible and capable of using common sense.

- No salary unless you've worked well this week.

- No marriage unless you've proven that you're committed, responsible, and can be trusted.

Whether we like it or not, life is full of consequences for behaviors—the connection between what we do and what we get is inevitable, natural, and a law of human nature. I'd much rather have a child learn the *if-then* connection at an early age, rather than later as an adult. However, there are those who don't seem to need the *then* part of the connection—kids who appear to be naturally compliant, responsible, and self-motivated. I suspect, though, that there is a subtle motivational system at work here. For example, "I'll do my homework as soon as I get home from school so Mom will be pleased" or "It's better to get the hard stuff over with first, *then* I can enjoy my evening." There's still an *if-then* connection, but it has become inculcated into the child's personality and has become second nature. And that is my goal when working with the *if-then student*—to reinforce the *behavior/consequence connection* so frequently that it becomes a natural part of the child's work ethic. Not only would Candice begin to take responsibility for completing her work in order to avoid negative consequences, but the positive feelings (the "atta girls" given by herself, her parents, and her teachers) would help to internalize appropriate study behaviors so that these would become second nature and self-rewarding. When that occurs, Candice's folks can relax, knowing that by external consequences "jump-starting" the process that Candice will have realized that academic achievement is rewarding unto itself.

2. The Chameleon Student

Chameleon students are some of the trickiest kids around. It's as if two, even three, children are inhabiting the same body. Have you ever watched a chameleon change colors, adapting to the limb he finds himself on, helping to ensure his survival? Well, so does the student version of a chameleon. These sneaky little critters adapt to teacher and parent expectations in hopes of surviving classes with the least amount of effort.

Jesse was such a kid—he could read a teacher like a book and scope out the situation by the end of the first day of school. In eighth grade, and therefore a pro at knowing the ins and outs of middle school, Jesse was very aware of which teachers stayed on top of their students' progress and those who were more lax. In prealgebra, his teacher gave a syllabus at the beginning of every grading period and stuck to it. The syllabus contained the daily homework assignments as well as test and quiz dates. There was no room for ambiguity and the teacher *collected and graded* each assignment on a daily basis. Since Jesse knew his work would be checked every day, he consistently did it and his math grades were good. Because he kept up with the work, tests made sense and were not beyond his grasp. Jesse's behavior in class was also appropriate, as this teacher sent home a bimonthly progress report noting each student's grade to date as well as behavior in the class. The progress report was to be signed by a parent and returned within three school days. If it was not returned, signed by a legitimate-looking parental signature, the parent was contacted by phone in order to set up a conference with the teacher. Jesse knew that he didn't have a crack to slip through in math class and therefore he kept the yakking to a minimum, watched his attitude in class, and completed all of his work.

However, history was another subject and a twig of a different color for this *chameleon student*. The history teacher was less organized—assigning tests and homework on a sporadic basis. Even when homework was assigned, kids swapped papers and graded each other's as the teacher read out the correct answers. It didn't take long for Jesse to realize that friends could "help out" and often he'd purposefully leave an answer blank so that a buddy could fill it in with the correct answer during the checking procedure. Because of this laissez-faire environment, Jesse slacked off in history—putting little effort into homework and counting on friends to help him out when the papers were scored.

However, quizzes and tests were tough for Jesse to manipulate. Since he didn't put much effort into his homework, exam questions rarely made sense to him—matching dates to historical events required memorizing the material and since he rarely studied or read the text, he usually had to guess at the answers and hope for the best. To compound the problem, two of his best friends sat near him in class and they tended to goof off constantly, not paying attention to the teacher's lectures and not taking class notes that were important preparation for the next quiz. Although the teacher requested that the three boys settle down, he rarely gave detentions and they tended to get away with their misbehavior. In short, Jesse's take on this class was easy to figure out—because of the teacher's loose style and lack of discipline Jesse took advantage of the situation. His behavior was disrespectful to the teacher and his attitude toward classwork and homework was to get by with as little as possible. Obviously he learned little from this situation and his grades were consistently poor.

When I met with Jesse and his folks following another report card showing an A in math and a D in history, I explained the *chameleon student* type of behavior that Jesse was evidencing. His parents readily agreed that their kid could read people and situations like tarot cards and he often tried this approach at home. Jesse would procrastinate with the chores his mother gave him, but would readily comply with his dad's request. Why? Because Dad was bigger, louder, and scarier than was Mom. This *chameleon student* didn't want to get Dad upset, as he was firm with his son and when he threatened a punishment for inappropriate behavior, he followed through with it. Mom, on the other hand, was a twig of a different color. Although she constantly nagged, threatened, and lectured Jesse, her words seemed to have little impact. Once in a while she'd follow through with the stated consequence, but most of the time she'd either shorten the restriction, give his bike back after just a few days, or even forget that he was supposed to be grounded from TV. Because of her inconsistency, Jesse preferred to gamble and to roll the dice—odds were that he'd get away with rude or irresponsible behavior with his mother, so he often took the chance. The same odds existed in history class, so he took advantage and slacked off. But with Dad and his math teacher (consistant and firm) he knew the limits and respected them.

This pattern is clear with *chameleon students*—they behave respectfully in environments that demand appropriate behavior and can be rude or irresponsible when they can get away with it in less demanding settings. *Chameleon students* are not bad kids—they just tend to take advantage of cracks in the situation and to slip through them whenever possible. If your child fits this profile, the trick is to anticipate the cracks (an ambiguous assignment schedule, a disorganized or even lazy teacher) and to make a plan for your child so that the manipulation is held down to a dull roar. Convince the teacher to sign off each day on your child's assignment sheet so that you'll know what's expected on a daily basis (more about this in Chapter Six). Check that the work gets turned in via mandatory bimonthly progress reports. Keep a close watch on your child's behavior by establishing open communication with the teacher via phone calls, notes, progress reports, or conferences. If your *chameleon student* sees that you're filling in the gaps by using these procedures, there will be little room for manipulation, rude behavior, or avoidance of school responsibilities.

3. The Disorganized Student

Middle school, generally beginning in the sixth grade, is often the acid test for many kids. While in grade school, most children have to deal with only one or two teachers a day and staying organized is easier. However, when kids find themselves responsible for six subjects (and therefore, six different teachers), many just can't seem to get it together. The math homework may be inadvertently stowed in the science folder and the geography text may not even make it to class because it was left in the locker.

Successfully navigating the ins and outs of middle and high school necessitates planning, organization, and staying on top of things. Marcus, a new client to my office, was obviously not doing a very good job of it. An average student in grade school, Marcus's grades had plummeted since beginning middle school the year before. He barely passed the sixth grade and his teachers had labeled him as somewhat of a slacker. In talking with his folks, I determined that Marcus fit into the category of the *disorganized student*, one who appears to be trying, but, just like Pigpen in the *Peanuts* comic strip, can't seem to keep things organized.

Marcus did his homework, but it was often incomplete and rarely did it get turned in on time. Since his math teacher gave assignments almost daily and would check them the next day, Marcus generally would attempt the work, but would either leave it at home or, if he did put it into his book bag, would have trouble finding it during class the next day. Marcus's locker was in even worse shape—he was missing his science book, but he had two copies of the health text. (His best buddy shared his locker at times and was just as disorganized! Often he would leave his own books and mistakenly take Marcus's from the locker.)

In my office, Marcus expressed surprise when his folks read me his latest progress reports—most of his teachers noted that he would be getting either D's or F's if he didn't start turning in his homework on time and studying for tests. Even his math teacher noted that several assignments had not been turned in. His parents swore they'd seen the work completed, in fact they'd actually done some of it for him! Marcus admitted that he would either forget to bring it to class or else was unable to find it after searching his backpack. He added that often he would find an assignment at a later date, but it would be too late to turn in to receive credit.

The *disorganized student* usually has good intentions—if they remember to write down their assignments and bring the necessary books home, there's a good chance that an attempt will be made to complete the work. Sometimes, though, only part of the assignment is written down and six hours later, sitting at the kitchen table, the child can't seem to remember the second part of the assignment. Frantic phone calls to friends may get results, but the end product is often incomplete. These kids are not lazy or rebellious, they just can't seem to get it together. They trust assignments to memory, share lockers with friends, stuff worksheets into their jeans pockets—all with the intention of sorting it out later. The problem is that the "sorting" rarely occurs. They truly are surprised when the worksheet is not where they remember putting it and must rack their brain trying to remember whose locker they left the science book in.

Parents are equally frustrated. Marcus's folks couldn't understand why he would take hours to carefully complete a homework assignment and somehow manage to misplace it. It just didn't add up and they were quickly losing patience with his absentmindedness. His mother had tried everything, she'd leave Marcus a note at breakfast instructing him to remember to pack his book bag correctly. Mom even put notes in his lunch bag to remind him to turn in his homework for fifth and sixth periods. These tactics were unsuccessful, as Marcus would read the note and became distracted by TV at breakfast or the lunch bag note would get thrown away with the remains of his sandwich.

Marcus's parents considered that he might have a memory or attention disorder, but a battery of psychological tests gave him a clean bill of health. There was nothing exotic that was wrong with Marcus—he just didn't have an organizational system that worked for him. He mistakenly trusted his memory or would write assignments on a slip of paper and shove it in the first available spot (pants pocket, bookbag, math text). He even tried writing assignments on his sneakers or the palm of his hand. Neither system worked, as his shoes would get scuffed or his palms would sweat and the note would become impossible to read.

How had this kid become so disorganized? Was he born like this or had he been allowed, or even encouraged, to develop such bad habits? In interviewing Marcus's folks, I heard the typical story of how kids end up so disheveled. It's usually a combination of nature (the genetic traits that you're born with) and nurture (what your environment teaches you). It's well known in the psychological literature that many personality traits are inborn and become apparent shortly after birth. Some are seen so early in life that genetics have to be given credit. Personality traits such as timidity, shyness, easy irritability, and others are known to be genetically based and can last a lifetime.

Perfectionism (or lack of) is also a personality trait that is seen to be genetically influenced, as well as being impacted by one's environment. Impulsivity is closely linked to heredity, as is distractibility. Marcus's father admitted that he had trouble as a child keeping things in order and if it wasn't for his older sister's help, he questioned whether he would have ever graduated from high school. His wife chimed in that Dad was known to leave things in the oddest places. She once found the cordless phone in the refrigerator and he was forever searching for his car keys. So Marcus's absentmindedness didn't fall far from the paternal tree. His mother felt that she'd contributed to the problem by doing everything for Marcus, even when he'd become old enough to be responsible for many of these tasks himself. She still woke him up in the morning, laid his clothes out the night before, and was constantly reminding him of things he had to do, rather than letting him be responsible for developing a reminder system himself. It appeared, therefore, that this kid was set up for failure by both genetics (his dad's absentmindedness) and nurture (his mom's overprotectiveness).

I explained to the family that we couldn't do anything about the genetic aspect, but we could sure change things on the home front. Marcus would have to learn to live by an academic organization system that was realistic and reasonable. His parents would need to externally motivate him daily by consistent usage of positive and negative consequences—rewards and punishments that actually mattered to him. Whether the organizational system would involve a state-of-the-art handheld computer, a daytimer, or a daily assignment sheet was not important. What mattered was that he would use a study skills system that his folks would stay on top of until Marcus could be trusted to handle it on his own.

Over the next few weeks I worked with Marcus and his family to set up my study skills program (as described in Chapter Six) and although there were some bumps in the road he quickly learned how to take responsibility for his assignments at school as well as chores at home. If Marcus could do it, anybody can!

4. The Manipulative Student

Unlike the *disorganized student*, who will do his homework (if he can remember the assignment and bring the books home), the *manipulative student* purposefully avoids doing her work. Cami, a high school sophomore, was a manipulative pro—she was proficient at using every trick in the book, telling her folks she'd completed her homework at school and had turned it in during class, announcing in a deceptively convincing voice that none had been assigned due to a daylong school assembly, or that she couldn't study for the history quiz because it was based on a series of videos shown during class and that there were no notes to study from.

Cami's folks weren't dummies—but they couldn't seem to catch her in the lies and fabrications. The kid was really good at it too—she seemed to have a ready and believable answer every day as to why she had little or no homework. They felt like they'd have to play detective in order to keep up with her excuses, calling the guidance counselor to see if there really was an assembly that day or whether math had a substitute for the entire week who didn't believe in giving homework. Cami even went as far as changing some grades on her report card. Once she used black ink to change a D to a B and an F to an A. Dad was fooled by the forgery, but Mom noticed the slight imperfection and confronted her. Cami stood her ground, swearing that the grades were legitimate, right until her folks marched her into the guidance counselor's office to check the grades on the computer. Only then, in the waiting room, did she crack and admit that she'd changed the report card. Cami didn't want to get in trouble with the school administrators by letting them know of her forgeries, so she reluctantly admitted to her parents that she had changed the report card.

When her parents told me of this, they were exasperated by her willful dishonesty and how far she would go to protect herself from having to face the consequences of her lies and dishonest behavior. I noted that if Cami would put even half of her planning and energy into actually doing her work that it would take less effort than all of the conniving, which was her current method of operation. It was as if Cami enjoyed manipulating her teachers and parents. She wasn't just trying to get out of doing classwork, homework, and studying—she also appeared to take pride in "getting something for nothing"—changing grades for her parents' review, copying friends' homework answers and turning these in as her own work to the teachers, and even cheating on tests.

When I spoke to Cami alone about her methods, she admitted that she wasn't learning much, but felt that she was beating the system, getting by with as little work as possible. Studying was for "dorks" as far as she was concerned. School was for socializing in class as well as in the hallways and academic work seemed like a nuisance rather than offering any positive benefit. According to Cami, only the naive kids actually studied and did their work. She and her friends were too smart to fall into that trap! Cami seemed proud of her ability to dupe her teachers and parents and the few times that it caught up with her didn't override the many instances in which she received credit by copying others' work, cheating on tests, or talking her way out of a bad grade (convincing her teacher she had turned the report in and that the teacher must have lost it).

Kids like Cami seem to delight in manipulation and take great pride in getting over on others. What Cami didn't realize, though, was that she would be the loser in the long run. Because she manipulated rather than studied, her knowledge was not keeping pace with her peers and she would have great difficulty passing the high school competency test necessary for graduation (meaning that even if she did earn enough credits to graduate, she'd not receive a regular high school diploma). Although Cami was a creative excuse-maker, her math was lousy and no amount of imaginative manipulation could take the place of good reading comprehension. She'd practically outmanipulated herself—sure she could fool her folks about homework, but it would be difficult to con her way into and through college.

Over the next year Cami would have to attend tutoring and night school classes to reinforce the information she'd missed due to her poor study habits. Not only would she have to attend day school (which she already disliked) but night school as well. Hopefully, her parents would check on her daily assignments and make sure that she was completing the work herself. This would be the only way in which Cami could prepare herself for the competency test—a big price to pay for her cunning, manipulative behavior.

5. The Here Today Gone Tomorrow Student

Josh's parents thought that they had it covered—Dad would drop his seventh grader off at school and wait until he walked into the building before leaving for work. Recently, however, Josh would turn around as soon as he saw Dad's car leave and hightail it to the convenience store across the street. There he'd meet up with at least one of his buddies and they'd make plans for the day. So far this semester they'd gone fishing at the creek and had spent a few days at a friend's house who lived close to the school and whose parents both worked, returning to the school grounds just in time to catch the bus home.

After the first grading period, Josh's parents noted the number of absences on the report card—seven—but they knew that he'd only missed school on two occasions due to illness. Josh was busted, and his mom and dad couldn't believe that he would skip school in the seventh grade! And even more distressing was their realization that he'd been able to miss school so many times without their knowledge.

What they didn't know was that Josh's school, like

many larger middle schools, had an automatic phone call system that dialed home the day after an absence and left a recorded message on the answering machine noting that the child had not been in school the day before. All Josh had to do was to beat Mom home, listen to the answering machine, and erase the message before she heard it. He even managed to beat the back-up system, which was a letter mailed home after the fifth absence. Josh would get the mail on his way up the driveway and dispose of the school's absentee notification letter before his folks could see it. The one glitch in the plan was the number of absences noted on the report card—Josh knew he couldn't talk his way out of that one, but chose to deal with it at the end of the grading period—after all, he was having too much fun skipping school with his friends to think that far ahead.

Once I was contacted by his folks about the truancy problem, we put a stop to it by using a daily sheet that all of his teachers had to sign each day. His parents were given a copy of each teacher's signature and if any of them looked suspicious on Josh's daily sheet, they would contact the school the next day, double-checking that he had been in class and that it was the teacher's actual signature. Josh's skipping days soon ended and even though his fishing suffered, his grades improved. Just knowing that his parents had access to daily communication with the school, and therefore daily confirmation of attendance, ended his truancy. Since he was now attending class, he knew what the homework was and he could appropriately prepare for tests and quizzes.

Luckily, Josh's folks got a handle on this behavior at an early stage. Truancy can easily become habitual, especially in high school aged kids. Then it's a behavior that's often difficult to break, especially when the youngster or his friends have cars for quick getaways and interesting outings!

6. The Rebellious Student

Once upon a time I had a dachshund named Willie. He started out as a graduation present from my husband and saw us through two houses, the birth of two kids, and the evolution of our careers. Willie had many fine points—a sleek coat, long snout, and a love for people. He was also the smartest dog I've ever heard of, evidencing more savvy than some folks I know.

But Willie had two dramatic flaws—he was stubborn and rebellious—not good traits to have when you mix them with doggie brilliance. Willie liked to do the opposite of what I requested (which meant that he was smart enough to understand what I wanted and then figure out how to go against it). When I would call him to come in, he would saunter away (although he probably would have preferred the air-conditioning to the hot Florida sun). Eventually his rebellious style not only got on my nerves, but almost led to his demise.

One morning I noticed a huge mound of freshly dug dirt piled next to a concrete slab in our backyard. Not thinking much about it (as Willie routinely dug up our backyard in an effort, I'm convinced, to make more work for us), I took a shovel and filled in the hole under the slab. I did notice that not all of the dirt went back in, but chalked that up to my sloppy shoveling and inability to pack the dirt down. A few hours later I noticed that Willie was nowhere to be found, and I had the chilling feeling that *he* was the reason that I couldn't get all of the dirt back where it belonged! I quickly dug out the hole and prodded under the slab with the tip of the shovel, searching for anything that resembled an obstinate dachshund. Then I felt it—the shovel lodged under a heavy but movable weight that I could lift a few inches. But since he was so far back under the concrete, I couldn't dig him out. You can imagine how horrible I felt—not only had I been known to curse this dog's obstinance, but now I had gone and done it—I had buried Willie alive! Now, how does one explain that to family and friends? I kept prodding and calling him to come out on the slight chance that he was still alive, but to no avail. There was no movement, no sign of life. After calling my husband at work and confessing my murderous sin, I got the bright idea that "We're just going to have to bury Willie anyway, so why not leave him where he is [it would be a secure site] and fill in the hole?" Sounded like a good idea at the time, so I headed back to the garage to retrieve the murder weapon (my trusty shovel) and to complete the act. Just as I rounded the corner to the backyard, I saw dirt coming out from under the slab and pretty soon Willie emerged, intact, seemingly no worse for wear. No one believed me, but I swear that he was wearing a doggie version of a smile, one of those "Ah-ha—boy did I pull one over on you" smiles! He bounded around the yard, joyous in the realization that he knew he'd won (you may think that I'm exaggerating—but, honest, that dog could play me like a fiddle!).

He had heard my calls, felt my prodding with the

shovel, but was darned if he was going to comply. Willie was a rebel with a cause—he understood exactly what I wanted, but spent most of his time plotting how to aggravate me. Yet not only did it almost kill him (I was ready to pack the dirt down *real well* the second time around), but his seeming nonsensical rebelliousness was a daily friction between us. And that's just dealing with a dog! When you have a child who's like Willie—smart, stubborn, and determined to avoid or disobey rules just for the heck of it— you've really got your hands full. And there's a bunch of them out there!

Rebellious students are passionate about doing whatever it takes just to spite you. At times it seems that they really wouldn't mind complying, but they just can't stand the feeling of not being the one who's in charge. They need to think that they're setting the rules (even if it would be the same rule that you would set) and they'll stoically accept all kinds of punishments to send their teachers or parents the message that they can't be forced to do anything, even if it happens to be something that they might enjoy. Their motto is "You can't make me"—and these kids have lost plenty of Beanie Babies, action figures, TV time, and other privileges just to prove that there's nothing you can do to get to them.

Why are these kids like this? Is it genetically or environmentally based? I honestly don't know, but I've had many parents of stubborn, rebellious kids confess that Grandma still reminds them of the countless whoopings and endless lectures given during their own rebellious childhoods. I bet that Willie's father was a bit obstinate too and that genetics does play a part in determining extreme stubbornness.

Let's take a look at the *rebellious student* in the classroom. Sammy fit the bill perfectly—only seven years old and he'd already accumulated quite a list of school problems. Sammy had been asked to leave three preschools prior to entering kindergarten. His folks had shown me the expulsion letters, which were all a variant of the same tune: "Sammy refuses to follow directions" . . . "He runs away from his teacher when called to come in from the playground" . . . "He cuts in front of others in line, pushing and shoving the children out of the way."

In kindergarten Sammy had trouble sitting on the circle line and raising his hand to be called upon. Although he knew one of the most important class rules was to wait his turn, whenever he knew the answer he'd blurt it out without giving the other kids a chance to answer. And to make matters worse, Sammy would refuse to sit on the time-out chair as punishment. His frustrated teacher tired of trying to coax him into time-out, just to have him take off as soon as she turned her back.

Sammy's folks had attended three conferences with the teacher and principal during his kindergarten year and first grade wasn't going much better. As he grew, so did his rebelliousness. Sammy's referrals often seemed random in nature—some days he didn't seem to mind doing certain tasks, yet other days he dug in his heels and no one could make him crayon if his life depended on it. Just like Willie, Sammy wanted to be the one in control, calling the shots. He seemed to put more energy into being negative and oppositional rather than having a plan for what it was that he really wanted. If Sammy was told to play with the blocks, he refused and fussed until allowed to put together a puzzle. Had he been offered the puzzle to begin with, he probably would have wanted the blocks. Sammy was a mess—he was miserable and so were those around him. Because he spent his time reflexively being rebellious, there was little energy and time left for enjoying the toys at school, playing with his friends, and especially learning. It's hard to focus on memorizing phonic rules or number sequences when you're worried about being first in line to lunch.

Completing classwork was out of the question, unless Sammy's first grade teacher was able to manipulate him into thinking that he had actually suggested the assignment. Although she'd successfully used this technique on a few occasions, Sammy was cagey and quickly caught on to her attempts to outmanipulate the manipulator. He was falling behind academically and his teacher was considering summer school as well as placing him in a special class for emotionally handicapped kids the next year in second grade.

Sammy's folks didn't want either of these options to occur, so they consulted with me about his rebellious behavior. After receiving a full history of Sammy's high jinks, it became clear that everyone had reacted to Sammy's stubbornness either by feeble attempts at punishments (five minutes in the time-out chair, where more often than not he'd leave prematurely) or by kicking him out of their program, as had happened in preschool. No one was sticking up to this kid, and by doing so they were not only allowing this inappropriate behavior to continue, but were actually encouraging it.

His parents and teacher were willing to do just about anything to gain a better balance in the situation. I explained that rebellious, controlling kids like Sammy need to feel that they have some say-so in their daily routines, but underneath the facade of the control freak, they're actually searching for adults to set limits and guidelines. They may fuss when these limits are first imposed, but time and again I find that these students actually respond well to and thrive upon fair limits. The trick is to let them feel that they have a choice in the outcome. For instance, if Sammy knew that not completing his morning classwork would *always* result in loss of recess (and having to spend that time in the classroom with the teacher's aide he'd probably choose to finish his assignments. It probably wouldn't work the first day, and maybe not even the first week, but eventually this bullheaded, *rebellious student* would give in because calling the shots (dawdling on his classwork) would not be worth the consequence (losing recess). And his parents would have to establish similarly tough consequences at home. Sammy might lose all electricity (television, Nintendo, radio, Game Boy, and so forth) if his teacher's daily report showed either uncooperative behavior or poor work completion. It would be Sammy's choice, and eventually he'd tend to become less rebellious and stubborn because the consequences would just not be worth it anymore. Sammy would change, but it would be the environment (his teacher and folks) that would have to externally motivate or jump-start such a process.

Rebellious students are a challenge to all, as well as being a disruption in the classroom. Once they see that they can control their environment by proper behavior, these stubborn students tend to become much more compliant and willing to flow with the program. Their true tendency toward bullheadedness probably remains, but they've learned to temper their behavior in order to gain control of their world in a more positive manner.

As a side note, remember my rebellious dachshund, Willie? Well, he lived several years past the day that I almost buried him alive. He was just two weeks shy of his sixteenth birthday when he died of old age. I have a feeling that's the way he planned it—still in control even until the end!

~~~~ Figure 1

Is Your Child an Underachiever?

Check out the following questions to help determine if your child is not working to her potential:

1. Does your daughter seem to get great grades in classes where she's held accountable for her work and the teacher is organized, yet seems to slack off with teachers who only check homework sporadically?

2. Does your son seem to procrastinate on homework assignments unless there's an activity offered as soon as he's completed it?

3. Does your child put off your requests unless there's something in it for him or else you threaten a punishment?

4. Do your kid's grades tend to vary with the crowd of children in his class? For instance, if there are lots of yakkers, does he join in and get detentions like the rest of them, yet remain quiet and respectful in classes where the teacher demands respect?

5. Does your child have terrific intentions each day of getting and staying organized, yet always seem to leave one important book or folder at school and therefore can't complete the homework?

6. Does your daughter seem scattered and forgetful, even about things that are very important to her? Is she frustrated by her own absentmindedness?

7. Is your son a pro at "omitting" important information, such as not telling you when book reports or projects are due, even though he has a steel trap for a memory when it comes to baseball statistics?

8. Does his "forgetting" about homework have a pattern—usually occurring on nights when a good TV show is on, but his memory improves radically when the TV is broken?

9. Does your child copy other's work, tests, and assignments and not seem to feel guilty about it?

10. Is your daughter missing classes, even whole days of school, without being ill? Do you find out about absences only when the school contacts you and she seems "puzzled" by the high number of missed days?

11. Have you overheard your child planning a "day off" from school without your permission, and when you ask about it, does she deny it?

12. Does your grade-schooler have a chip on his shoulder and carry a grudge if he's been annoyed by the teacher? Will he "cut off his nose to spite his face" just to show the teacher that he doesn't care about math class (even though he's a math wiz!)?

13. Does your middle-schooler detest regulations and challenge not only you and your home rules, but the teacher and class rules as well?

If you answered *yes* to at least seven of these questions, then your child is probably not working to her ability. Don't worry, you can get her back on track by following the guidelines of my study skills program!

three

The Six Mistakes Even
Savvy Parents Make

~~~~~~

Just as there are individual styles of underachieving children, parents tend to have individual patterns of mistakes they make in dealing with their kids. Generally, we respond to our children's underachieving behavior based upon how our own parents dealt with similar issues. If you tended to be a responsible student, most likely your parents took a backseat and let you call the shots. That works well when kids are motivated—they seek out their parents only for specific help on math problems or large projects, but in the main they take care of their day-to-day work themselves. If your daughter is like you were (responsible and self-motivated), then most likely you can follow your parents' pattern and let her lead the way. The problem occurs, however, if she's different—perhaps procrastinating and letting work slip until the last minute or is disorganized or forgetful. A laissez-faire attitude won't work with this type of child and you'll need to use a different tactic.

Too often, though, we tend to react to our children not as individuals—but more reflexively, either mimicking our own parents' tactics if we felt comfortable with the memories or perhaps rebelling and doing the opposite of what we experienced if our childhood memories were less than pleasant. The problem with both of these scenarios is that in neither case are we taking into account the individual needs and behavior of our own children. Setting up a rigid study schedule for an organized, responsible student may be overkill—it's not necessary and may actually interfere with the child's achievement as well as love of learning. On the other hand, employing a sink-or-swim academic philosophy with a lazy, manipulative, or disorganized kid is tantamount to setting him up for failure. Just because your folks let you determine whether to study or not doesn't mean that this tactic will be successful with your kid. Forget the old tapes—try not to fall into the trap of mimicking or doing a one-eighty based upon how you were raised. What's important is determining your child's individual style and reacting appropriately with an effective plan.

I've seen six mistakes commonly made by many parents when dealing with child underachievement—you may find yourself guilty of making one or more of these errors. The six mistakes to watch out for are:

• Peace at Any Price

• Leave It to the Teacher

- The Denial Dance
- Doing the Homework for Your Child
- Over Committing Kids
- Unreasonable Expectations

Mistake #1: Peace at Any Price

Craig and Sherry had many things in common when they married—education, religious beliefs, financial goals, and a mutual dislike of confrontation. They initially gravitated to each other because they were low-key people, tending to avoid arguing, compromising readily, and being pretty darn good at negotiating. If Sherry was upset with Craig for forgetting an important date, he would quickly apologize and she was accepting. As neither spouse liked to argue, they found it easier to give in on most disagreements and this seemed to work for them in their marriage. However, the cooperative balancing act that they had established so eloquently in their marriage was upset when they became parents to strong-willed, stubborn Nicholas.

It was easy to placate Nick as a baby, when he became frustrated, Sherry would try to decipher his needs and to gratify him immediately. When Nick was tired or hungry, Craig rushed to lie down with him or to feed the baby Over the years, though, Craig and Sherry noticed that Nick was evolving into a bit of a tyrant. In order to avoid his fits and fussing, they quickly catered to his whims, not wanting Nick to have to endure frustration—and themselves not wanting to endure the noise. In the preschool years it just seemed easier to give in to Nick rather than to discipline him. Both grandmothers, who were of the old school, warned the parents that Nick was taking the terrible two's a little too far and that the child was being spoiled. Craig and Sherry knew in their hearts that their mothers were right, but they just didn't have the guts to stand up to their son, nor the stamina to listen to his fussing, even if he was placed in time-out for a few minutes.

Things came to a head, though, when Nick entered grade school. He treated his kindergarten teacher as he had his parents and he would pull a meltdown if he didn't get his way. If the teacher asked the class to sit at their desk and do seat work, Nick generally began to fool around, distract others, or would refuse to comply. It was on one of Nick's especially bad days that I first came into contact with the family. I was observing another child in the class, one who was having trouble socializing with her peers. During the hour visit, my attention was constantly drawn to Nick—at times he was rude to the teacher and his classmates, would leave his seat to ramble around the room, and completed very little of his seat work. This kid was a mess, and I wasn't surprised when the teacher informed me that she was referring Nick and his folks to my office.

It was only a few minutes into our first interview that I realized that Nick's parents had made the classic mistake of accepting *peace at any price* as a parenting technique with their child. Their history of placating Nick, his growing intolerance for frustration, and his rude behavior at school were symptomatic of this very common parental error. What begins as a dislike of limit-setting around the house for fear that the child may become upset, unhappy, or angry usually generalizes into the classroom. Kids who do not learn compliance behaviors at home also lack self-discipline within the classroom. Because home rules can be hazy, ambiguous, or changeable (depending upon the decibel level reached during a tantrum), the child often cannot deal with firm and strict classroom rules. The parents' mistake of accepting *peace at any price* (avoiding confrontation by giving in) teaches the youngster to try the same tactics at school. If refusal, screaming, or threatening to be unhappy work with Mom and Dad, why wouldn't the same tactics be successful at school?

Makes sense, with the exception that teachers rarely put up with this type of behavioral malarkey. They have twenty or so kids to deal with on a daily basis and just don't have the time or patience for one child who feels that he's above the rules. The parental mistake of accepting *peace at any price* is rarely duplicated in the classroom and often these kids are found to be disliked and even ostracized by their peers for their inappropriate behavior. And that's exactly what was happening to Nick—after only four months of kindergarten, his classmates rarely included him in games because he was so bossy and they tired of his fussing when he didn't get his way. Classmates won't make the mistake of *peace at any price*—they just shun the child, writing him off as a nuisance.

When I explained to Sherry and Craig that their parenting style of taking the easy way out could actually cause Nick severe behavioral and emotional problems, they seemed shocked. They felt that *they* were the victims, having been abused by his tyrannical ways for years. I showed them, though, that Nick was the real victim in the long run. They avoided his meltdowns by giving in to his every whim, but teachers and classmates would not. He was already behind academically because he had not been taught to persevere when frustrated, he just gave up and would throw his pencil down when the task became too challenging. Doing homework was generally out of the question also. If Nick didn't feel like practicing his letter sounds as assigned by his teacher, he just refused and his folks would give up and let him watch TV. In class, because most of the other children were better prepared and had completed the work, Nick began to feel left out, would complain that he felt stupid, and that nobody liked him. Nick wasn't stupid—far from it. He was *unskilled* because he refused to complete his classwork and homework. Consistently being academically unprepared can make a child feel stupid and out of place. Nick's self-concept was suffering because he was embarrassed when peers could do academic tasks that he wasn't prepared for. Also, being rejected is no fun, and even though he continued with his bossy ways, Nick didn't understand why he wasn't invited to parties or asked to join in games at recess.

So the mistake of *peace at any price* actually has a tremendous price tag attached to it. How can we measure the cost of a weak academic foundation, poor self-concept, and inappropriate coping skills? In raising kids there is no free lunch—you generally get what you pay for. Parents who are afraid of confronting child misbehavior pay dearly for years, as the kid becomes more tyrannical and out of control. But as can be seen in Nick's case, the child is the one who ultimately suffers the most. At least Nick was only in kindergarten when the teacher put her foot down. With counseling and much guidance, Sherry and Craig would be able to get Nick back on track. But first, they would have to accept that *peace at any price* is really an oxymoron. The peace is fleeting and the price that is paid by giving in to tantrums is harmful to everyone—the child, parents, teachers, and classmates. There is no substitute for teaching children self-discipline and it is only when the child can tolerate frustration and to persevere even when challenged will he be able to learn to his potential.

Mistake #2: Leave It to the Teacher

Almost as frequently as the *peace at any price* mistake is the error of assuming that just because you haven't heard anything from the teacher that your child is on target academically. With today's large classes, it's tough for a teacher to communicate with all of the parents, even if she were motivated to do so. Some enlightened school districts or individual teachers have set up systems to help keep parents abreast of assignments, though. The most successful systems I've seen are:

- Students receiving weekly or monthly calendars stating when assignments or projects are due and when tests or quizzes will occur. To be effective, the teacher's presentations should stay current with their calendar so that it remains accurate.

- A telephone voice-mail hot line that is updated each day by each teacher. Parents and students can call to confirm if a test was announced that day and when the next assignment is due.

- An Internet e-mail system updated daily by each teacher, working similarly to the voice-mail system noted above.

- The old-fashioned, but still very effective, homework assignment sheet that the student fills in with all homework, tests, quizzes, and projects announced that day. This is most effective if all teachers initial it daily, validating the accuracy of the information.

As can be seen—whether the system is technologically advanced (voice-mail, e-mail) or involving only a sheet of paper, the goal is the same—that each day teachers communicate their expectations to the parents. Of course, it's up to the student (and the parents in many cases) to see that the work is completed. There is really no excuse for a lack of daily communication between school and home. Monthly and even weekly progress reports often don't cut it—all they do is document what your child hasn't turned in and often it's too late to get the work done at that time in order to receive credit for it.

Parents who assume that "no news is good news" are often making the second mistake, falling into the *leave it to the teacher* syndrome. They assume (which can be quite risky when it comes to dealing with kids and academics) that they'll be contacted immediately if there's either a behavioral or academic problem. In my experience, teachers are apt to notify parents if the child is acting up and disturbing the class, but are less communicative when it comes to academic difficulties.

This is not to suggest that your child's teacher doesn't care about his underachievement—it's just easier to let that slip through the cracks when more urgent issues demand their attention. For example, the teacher can't ignore fighting behavior or sexual harassment issues—these are potentially dangerous and in today's litigious world often take precedence over academic issues. Teachers rarely get sued for children not working to their potential, but just the thought of being accused of ignoring a sexual harassment complaint sends chills down the spines of many school administrators.

In addition, many teachers have been conditioned to parental apathy. Just go to a PTA meeting and notice the turnout. Generally only a small percentage of available parents attend and those who do show up are the "regulars" who are usually not the parents of underachieving or disruptive children. The latter parents rarely, if ever, attend—either due to work conflicts, not even knowing about the PTA meeting, or indifference about school. Over the years many teachers come to the conclusion that it's up to the parent to track them down and to show interest, rather than vice versa. I sympathize with these professionals—they have been disappointed so often by parental apathy that they come to avoid communication with the home, as it generally is not reciprocated by the parents.

There is an interesting trend, though, in a new model of education—the fundamental school. (Actually, this is a revival of old school methods, but is seen as new to today's parents.) In fundamental schools the children are allowed to remain only if their families are represented at *all* PTA meetings, a parent must sign the assignment sheet daily, and *all* homework must be turned in to the teacher each day. Fundamental school administrators are not fooling around. They only want families who are involved and committed to the child's education and if the family is not up to snuff, they get the proverbial shoe. My first impression of this system was that it's rather harsh and rigid, yet statistics show the following results of fundamental school placements:

- Higher standardized test scores

- Excellent parental involvement not only at mandatory meetings but also at extracurricular events

- An extremely low attrition rate—somehow these parents make it to the meetings, sign the daily assignment sheets, and make sure that Junior's homework gets turned in the next day

- The teachers tend to be available and responsible to parental concerns—they are involved with the family and appreciate the open communication

One may propose that only a certain type of family can maintain this degree of involvement—Mom may be a stay-at-home mother, the family can afford a babysitter in order to volunteer at the school, or that the parents are highly educated themselves in order to guarantee that all homework assignments can be completed. In many cases this is true, but I've known several families who rise to the occasion by rescheduling work hours to fit in with the PTA schedule, they turn off the television and actually miss out on some of their favorite shows in order to supervise the child's homework, and they genuinely change their priorities so that school comes first. These individuals are not necessarily well-educated, wealthy, or have nannies to help out—they've committed themselves to becoming involved in their child's education. At first it's often tough to rearrange schedules, but once they get the hang of it, it works.

These folks should be congratulated, but what about the large group of parents who make the *leave it to the teacher* mistake? There are two forms of *leave it to the teacher* patterns that I see in my practice. First, some families assume that they will be contacted by the teacher if there's a problem with their child's grades. If they are contacted, though, these folks then become involved and devote the time to making sure that the work gets done and turned in. Their problem was just not knowing what was expected of their child on a daily basis.

Matthew's folks made this type of error. His parents were fuming when I met them at our first session—Mom was appalled that he had received a nine-week report card with two B's, two C's, and two D's. The parents had not received any warning notices from either of his third grade teachers about the D's in science and social studies and wanted my opinion as to how to confront the teachers on this point. They admitted that they checked Matthew's bookbag only once a week—on Friday, in order to throw out any spoiled food items he'd inadvertently left in lunch bags, and they usually just asked him each day how every-thing had gone and if he had completed his homework. His usual response was "fine" to the first question and "yes" to the second.

When I spoke alone with Matthew, he admitted to me that he had received midterm progress reports regarding the potential D's, but had ditched them in the trash before his folks could find them. He also noted that not all of his homework had been completed each day, especially in those two subjects. Matthew complained that he didn't like the teacher and that his assignments often necessitated reading the chapter in order to find the answers for the worksheets.

When I sat down with the family, Matthew finally fessed up to his crimes, and his folks were relieved that they had not confronted the teachers with erroneous allega-tions. They were disappointed in Matthew's deception (throwing the progress reports away), but still felt that a phone call from the teacher had been in order. Now that they knew that they needed to double-check his work on a daily basis, they felt confident that they could follow through with it. Mom and Dad admitted to making the *leave it to the teacher* mistake of expecting immediate teacher contact and vowed to keep much closer tabs on their son. They agreed they would become a team with Matthew and all of his teachers, making sure that he was on track, setting up an assignment sheet system and completing his work each day.

I felt confident that Matthew and his folks would suc-ceed—now that they had identified the problem as a lack of daily information in regard to teacher expectations, they could do their part by making sure that these responsibilities would be fulfilled. Matthew was less than pleased, as this meant doing more homework and playing less, but he resigned himself to the situation and I'm sure he adapted soon.

The second type of *leave it to the teacher* mistake takes it one step further than just not knowing what is due each day. Not only do parents who make this mistake assume that "No news is good news," but further the error by removing themselves almost totally from the picture by expecting the teacher to remedy the problem once they find out that it does exist. Melissa's father, a single parent who worked long hours and hadn't been a particularly responsible student himself in high school, believed that since her ninth grade teachers were getting paid by his tax money that not only should they be teaching his daughter, but they also should be responsible for ensuring that she completed and turned in her homework, as well as adequately preparing her for tests and quizzes.

When he finally received her report card (she had "forgotten" about it until after the homecoming dance), Melissa's father grounded her for the D in English and the F in algebra. Melissa had threatened to run away if he stuck to the restriction and her father worried that she might actually do so. Her school counselor was concerned with Melissa's anger and depressed attitude and had suggested that they meet with me to diagnose the severity of the problem and to try to work out a solution. The school counselor felt that antidepressant medication might be in order and wanted my opinion.

After talking to Melissa and her father individually, it

was evident that a *pill* wouldn't solve this problem—it wasn't a medication issue, it was a poor study habit/Dad-daughter relationship problem. Melissa had never been particularly enthusiastic about school, but had generally kept up with her work, slipping here and there. She managed to work harder in subjects with lower grades during the next six weeks so that everything averaged out to at least a C by the end of the semester. Somehow, though, English and algebra had gotten out of hand and she was truly surprised that her grades had slipped to a D and an F. Melissa was evidencing a *situational depression*—feeling sad and blue, but with good reason to feel this way. Kids *should* feel bad when they are restricted and can't hang out with their buddies and it gets lonely and boring on weekends with only their folks to talk to (it's when kids get depressed for no obvious reason that I begin to worry).

I discussed the situation with *both* Melissa and her father and described to them the roles *both* of them had played in this academic mess. Melissa had acted irresponsibly—doing the minimum amount of work just to get by in her classes, miscalculating, and letting too many assignments go undone or poorly completed. Apparently ninth grade required more effort than did middle school and she was learning this the hard way. Dad also was in error. His *leave it to the teacher* attitude obviously wasn't going to cut it in high school. The teachers, often having twenty-five or more students, six periods a day, couldn't take responsibility for making the kids do their work. Their job was to teach the material, assign homework and announce tests, and be available to those students who requested extra help. They were also responsible for being available to parents who wanted to work out a system of communicating daily assignments, but that meant that the parents would have to be involved by checking that the work was completed each day. Melissa's father honestly wanted nothing to do with either of these tasks—he just wanted Melissa to make good grades via some combination of student-teacher effort. Dad was still searching for the easy way out, some type of "motivational pill" that he could pop into his daughter's mouth each day that would somehow make her stay on task and complete the math problems.

When I confronted them with the errors each had made, Melissa was actually the more responsive of the two. She knew that she had screwed up, acting irresponsibly by trying to get by doing the minimum amount of work. However, she still was angry about the restrictions that her father had imposed and wanted to work out a compromise. Dad was a tougher cookie to deal with—he was overwhelmed by his own busy work schedule and resented having to become involved with Melissa's academics. Why couldn't she just handle it herself? I explained to him that the bottom line was that as unfair as it seemed, Melissa needed his intervention. For a variety of reasons, she was not adequately motivated and was poorly prepared and disorganized. Melissa needed to know that her father was going to check her work each day, and just by knowing this, she would most likely do a better job of staying on top of her assignments herself. Dad shouldn't expect the teachers to do it—the buck stopped with he and Melissa, like it or not. I suggested working out a behavioral management study habits program that involved Melissa completing all work each day with Dad checking it. Instead of the lengthy

restriction he had imposed, they agreed to a daily consequence system that made more sense, was fair, and that
both could live with. Melissa's mood immediately improved and Dad no longer had an angry and sulky kid to
deal with. The trick would be keeping up with the system
and I warned her father that if he backed out again, making
the *leave it to the teacher* mistake, that Melissa may revert to
her old irresponsible ways.

In both Matthew's and Melissa's cases, their folks had
made faulty assumptions—that the teachers would keep
them closely informed about academic problems and, additionally in Melissa's case, that they would also solve them. I
imagine that in some very special academic settings teachers may perform these functions, but in most schools the
leave it to the teacher concept just doesn't cut it.

Mistake #3: The Denial Dance

One of the toughest academic mistakes for me to work
with is that of the parent in denial. Generally, two behaviors need to occur for the *denial dance* to occur. First, the
parents have to put the child on a pedestal—feeling that
the kid is above deception and manipulation and that the
child is about as close to perfection as a kid can be. The parents must feel in some manner that if their child fails, makes
a mistake, or displays any problems, this is a direct reflection
upon the parent, "If my kid is irresponsible, then somehow
I am irresponsible and that can't be . . . therefore the ac-
cuser must be wrong." Convoluted logic, but many folks
doing the *denial dance* actually think like this. They're not a

whole lot of fun to deal with in therapy either: "I'm here because the private school threatened to expel Yvonne due to poor grades . . . if she has poor grades, it's because they're doing something wrong . . . therefore, they should be the ones coming to therapy." It's tough to deal with people who think like this, as the logic is so irrational that they just don't get it, nor do they want to.

The second factor in the *denial dance* mistake is the kid. She must be aware of her parents' defensiveness, appreciate how she can use it to get out of a pickle, and have at least minimal acting skills in order to go in for the kill effectively. Twelve-year-old Katye was up for the part—she had figured out as early as preschool that her folks would run interference for her if she was blamed for misbehavior—either at school, a party, or at a friend's house. When I interviewed her, she struck me as a cagey kid who had learned to play her parents like a fiddle. Both Gina and Howard had doted on their daughter, sending her to private school and enrolling her in ballet as well as weekend theater classes. Not only were they proud of her accomplishments, but vicariously saw her successes as their own achievements. If Katye wasn't invited to a party, *they* felt rejected and rather than figure out why their daughter was being rebuffed (possibly having something to do with her behavior?), they immediately became defensive, launching into what was wrong with the birthday girl's character or family dynamics.

Because of her parents' defensiveness and tendency to deny faults in their daughter, Katye grew up believing that she was above the rules. Notes from her teacher describing disruptive, noncompliant behavior were either dismissed by her parents or they would angrily confront the teacher, demanding an apology. Their child couldn't have started a food fight, she *must have been provoked*! This defensive attitude, based upon the mistake of denying that Katye just might have some faults in the areas of behavior and responsibility, led to several school changes, since few teachers would apologize for Katye's irresponsible or disruptive behavior. And as the years went by, both the parents and the child continued in this dance of denial, Katye's folks running interference while she sat on the sidelines watching them do battle for her!

At age twelve and in the sixth grade, Katye's folks were in my office because they were running out of private schools to send her to. Three of her six teachers at her current school were fed up—she constantly chatted in class, had to have the last word when she was asked to quiet down, and her academic work had become spotty. The headmaster had assigned detentions and Saturday school, but Katye's parents did not encourage her to pay the consequences for her behavior, since they believed that the teachers were wrong by trying to "break her spirit" (stop the yakking in class) or were expecting too much of her (by doing classwork and homework on a consistent basis). The school was considering expulsion for the entire family and since they had run out of other options (public school was seen as unacceptable to Katye's folks), they were resigned to making this situation work. Gina had heard from friends that I had worked closely with this school and was desiring to "hire" me to persuade the headmaster to give Katye another chance. Gina, obviously, was still denying that Katye had the problem—she wanted the teachers and administration to see the error of their ways. Needless to say, Gina was less than pleased when I informed the family that in my opinion the school was right. Their rules and expectations were reasonable—twelve-year-olds should be able to resist yakking, can pay attention to the teacher, be polite, and complete academic assignments. It was Katye who would have to change—to knock off the misbehavior and to improve her academic production.

I truly believe that if Howard and Gina had other school options for Katye that would have been my last conversation with them. Since the consequence of expulsion (attendance at, in their opinion, an inferior private school or public school) was out of the question, they chose the lessor of two evils—working with me. This was not an easy task, since neither party (Katye and her folks, nor I) genuinely wanted to work with each other. But we all rose to the challenge, Gina because she had to in order to save Katye from the perceived horrors of public school and myself because this was my job.

Over the next few weeks we had several sessions together and more progress was made than I had expected. Because I focused on Katye's behavior (talking out, completion of classwork), rather than on her character (impolite, spoiled, disrespectful), Gina and Howard could handle it. We set up a system to receive daily behavioral and academic performance reports from each teacher, which also included Katye's assignments for the next day. Her parents gave her positive or negative consequences daily, depending upon the quality of the teacher's reports. Katye saw the system as fair and responded well to it, and her folks slowly became believers that the teachers really didn't have it out for the kid, but that they had been frustrated by Katye's previous misbehavior. They were even becoming complimentary now that Katye was making both behavioral and academic progress. I'm not kidding myself into thinking that the *denial dance* was broken—they still performed it in other areas, but at least in terms of schoolwork and behavior, Howard and Gina had become more realistic about their daughter.

Parents who are in denial of their kid's misbehavior or poor study habits are also denying their child the chance to change—if room for improvement is not felt to be necessary, then none will occur. It's tough to admit to the mistake of doing the *denial dance*—but perhaps you can see some traits in yourself of the overprotective, defensive style that Gina and Howard portray. And trust me, if you're doing the dance, your child will zero in and take advantage—by blaming others for her failures as well as refusing to take responsibility for her own actions.

Mistake #4: Doing the Homework for Your Child

Many of us have had the not-so-fond childhood memory of sitting at the dinner table for what seemed to be hours on end, staring at the peas or broccoli getting colder by the minute after having been informed by our parents that "You will not leave this table until every one of those peas is eaten." We were determined not to lose the food war— at least I was. There must have been some principle at stake—pride at the very least—and I was darned if a single pea would be consumed. What I counted on was that my mother would not keep me there all night long and that at some point she'd give up and send me to my room. At least there I could walk around and not have to stare at disgusting stuff on my dinner plate. It always worked—at some point she'd clear the table and although I was banished to my bedroom, I had gotten away with not consuming a single pea! A victory of sorts, I suppose, and to this day I do not inflict peas upon my own kids.

What does pea-eating have to do with academic underachievement? Well, actually, nothing—but there is an appropriate analogy here. It involves the child's uncanny ability to sit for extended periods of time doing nothing, just to avoid completing an unpleasant task. Normally kids can't sit still very long when bored, but it becomes a different ball game when it involves avoidance of a nasty task, whether it's eating vegetables or doing homework.

That's why I had so much compassion for Zach—a first grader who was on his way to breaking records for sitting at the kitchen table staring into space instead of copying his spelling words five times each. His parents complained that they dreaded Monday nights—the day the new list of spelling words came home from the teacher. Getting Zach's homework done became a family trauma—Monday night he was supposed to copy the words, Tuesday he was to use them in a sentence, Wednesday night to define orally what each word meant, and on Thursday night to review the spelling again. Ten words—his parents reported—a task that could easily be completed within fifteen minutes per day.

And on top of the spelling homework, Zach often had

math to do—not much, but to complete five or ten single-digit addition problems, another ten-minute task at max. This total of twenty to thirty minutes of assignments, though, often lasted for hours, with Zach either staring blankly into space, laying his head down on the table, falling out of the chair onto the floor, or whining and fussing. The bottom line was that very little homework was getting done. Zach's father tried sitting with him in order to motivate performance, but this seemed to work only when he gave Zach the answer. When Dad left the table, his son would revert to staring, whining, daydreaming, or doodling—but not getting his work done.

It wasn't long before Zach had trained his father into doing most of his work for him. Dad would "show" Zach how to do the addition problem, Zach would pretend to "listen" and would perk up when his father quit explaining how to add the two numbers together and finally just gave him the answer. The end product was that Dad's spelling and single-digit addition were improving and Zach's math pages and sentences were completed, but the child was learning very little.

However, Zach was learning to become "helpless," to depend upon his folks to give him the answers, to quit when the work became tedious or laborious, and to manipulate his responsibilities. His father was unintentionally sending the message that it's okay to give up when challenged and he was also confirming Zach's feeling that perhaps he wasn't smart enough to do first grade work after all. Zach was plenty smart—he was just a bit lazy and fearful of failure. Having his father do his homework for him not only rewarded his laziness, but Zach sensed that even his dad felt that the work was too hard for him. And because he wasn't doing it himself, Zach wasn't practicing the words or math concepts and was falling behind in school. By February, his teacher put the family on notice that Zach's name was being placed on the possible retention list and that he could be held back if he didn't learn the concepts at an adequate rate by the end of the school year.

The concept of grade retention came as a shock to all and that's what precipitated a visit to my office. Zach told me that he'd be embarrassed if he was held back in first grade and his folks were frustrated because they knew that their son could do the work—they just didn't have the patience to make him. It had become easier to do it for him, Zach seemed happier and the endless hours of whining or dawdling at the kitchen table had ceased. The trade-off, though, was that Zach wasn't learning the work, and just as important—the self-discipline to force himself to complete it. I suggested that we try some new tactics to help put Zach into control of his homework completion and to boost his self-confidence.

The possibility of repeating first grade was a distinct motivator for Zach. He was willing to work with me on a new study skills program. His parents, having learned the mistake that doing homework for a child actually teaches him to perceive himself as helpless, were willing to do anything. I suggested that we try to make homework time more fun by instituting the following procedures:

- Use a timer to play "beat the buzzer." If Zach finished the work on time, he received a treat or a token as a reward.

- Break down the amount of work into smaller parts and intersperse easier homework tasks or a few minutes of fun time before beginning the next assignment.

- Deciding what task to tackle first by writing assignments on small slips of paper and having Zach randomly pull one from a jar. After completing the first, he would pull another slip out to determine what he would work on next.

Zach's folks were told to be available to offer help, not answers, when he really needed it, but not to sit with him trying to coax him into doing his work. If he wasn't cooperative that night (if he didn't try to beat the buzzer, wouldn't pull a slip of paper from the jar), the work was taken away after a set amount of time and Zach was dismissed from the table. He was not allowed to play outside or to use any type of electricity that evening (television, Game Boy, CD player, and so forth). In addition, Zach would have to go to school the next day empty-handed. His parents would arrange with the teacher that Zach would lose recess if his homework had not been turned in. This double dose of consequences (at home and at school the next day) was very potent—Zach hated being restricted at home as well as losing recess at school, knowing that his friends were outside playing foursquare or tag. On the other hand, he really enjoyed playing "beat the buzzer" and became somewhat of a miser with the tokens he won, saving up for a remote-control car.

The system was not perfect, and Zach did spend some time on restriction, but most days he managed to complete his work in a timely fashion. His folks, especially his father, reported that it seemed more difficult for them to change *their* behavior and to not do the work for their son than it was for Zach to change his behavior. But the threat of grade retention hovered over their heads and they learned to restrain themselves, letting Zach complete his own work. Zach slowly became more confident of his abilities and began to ask for help only when he really needed it.

Zach will make it into second grade, but only because his folks stopped the helplessness cycle—if the child dawdles or fusses, it's easier to give him the answer, which leaves the child unprepared, lowers his self-concept, and teaches the wrong lesson in terms of self-discipline. The *do the homework for the child* mistake is indeed insidious—it starts out in an effort to jump-start the homework process, but often ends up sabotaging acquisition of healthy study habits.

Mistake #5: Overcommitting Kids

Work begins at 7:30 A.M. with a thirty-minute lunch break and continues until 2:30 P.M. Most afternoons there are meetings until 5:00 or 5:30, then time to rush home or drive through for a quick dinner, then off to a second job for a few hours. What a day—no wonder you're pooped out by 8:00 P.M.! But you, the adult, are not whom I'm talking about—it's your child!

Many kids I know, including my own at times, have lived by this schedule, only that "work" is school, the "afternoon meetings" are really baseball or softball practices, and the second job (doing homework) occurs after the drive-through at McDonald's. No wonder our kids are worn out by evening, just in time to start their homework. They muddle through it, often skipping the items necessitating creative thought, and rarely have the energy or motivation to call a friend for help on a particularly tricky problem. Then it's lights out about 11:00 or 11:30 P.M. and back up by 6:40 the next morning. No wonder these kids are underachieving—they're working on only four cylinders, rather than on all eight. And it's not just the high schoolers who tend to overdo it. I've met grade-schoolers who need a daytimer just to keep their schedules in order!

In our efforts to be the best parents we can be, sometimes we overdo it—trying to give our children opportunities that we didn't have in hopes that they'll pick up a lifelong skill or hobby (golf or tennis), become more agile and self-confident (ballet or karate), or hit like Mark McGwire via Little League practice. We are certainly well intentioned and sometimes even our children actually like the activity. My daughter went through several types of lessons over the years before we finally hit on one that *she* truly enjoyed. First came ballet, then gymnastics, followed by tennis, art class, back to tennis again, soccer, snorkeling, violin, piano, swimming, jazz, roller skating, ice skating, basketball, and softball. Oh, did I mention a yearlong stint of horseback-riding lessons, and I almost forgot—several years of Girl Scouts? That's sixteen—count them, seventeen if tennis counts twice. Some of these activities she enjoyed at times, whereas others she just put up with. My theory had been that you can't like something until you're good at it, but she proved to me that in her case, at least, the opposite was true—she wasn't going to be good at something unless *she* liked it. And that turned out to be softball—begun in fourth grade and continuing still in college!

Many of us fall into the trap of trying to stimulate our kids, and if kept in the right perspective, it can be a positive and fun experience. Listening to her violin attempts were painful to all, but I was determined that she would have music in her life, just as I had when I was a kid (my mother had attended Julliard and could play piano with the best of them). My daughter still has music in her life—a tape player in her car and lots of CDs at home. She's not performing, thank heavens, and we all have come to appreciate that!

There's nothing wrong with exposing your child to sports, music, dance, or martial arts—but the key I've learned is to keep it to a healthy balance. Kids really have two missions in life—doing a good job with schoolwork and enjoying some free play time. If extracurricular activities do not interfere too much with either, they are probably a good idea. If, however, the balance tips from *exposing* the kid to *overwhelming* her, then perhaps some of the extra activities should be put on the back burner for a while.

It's important to keep your individual child's personality, time constraints, and abilities in perspective. Some kids thrive on baseball—that's play to them and they're content to do well at school as well as on the diamond. It's the kid who changes clothes (in the car) right from school to make it to karate on time, eats (in the car) on the way to piano, and completes homework—yes, in the car—in order to get to Scouts who may be overburdened. Something has to give and it's usually schoolwork. It's difficult to try your best when fitting in math problems between activities or to really comprehend the science chapter with your little brother babbling away in the car seat next to you.

If this sounds like your child's schedule, take a moment to prioritize. Ask him what he likes and doesn't like about each activity (academics aren't in this drill—these are mandatory!). Even if he loves everything that he's doing, his time may be unbalanced. The red flags to look for are:

- hurrying through homework and studying for tests

- sagging grades in school

- tired in the morning upon wakening and exhausted by bedtime

- irritable and moody

- anxious—feeling as if he can't quite get everything in

If two or more of these conditions exist, you may have to insist upon lightening his schedule, always keeping homework and study time as the primary activities. It's tough to think of extracurricular activities as a parental mistake, but your child may become too overwhelmed to work to his academic potential. Even though you're well intentioned, the end result may just not be worth it. I've learned (the expensive and hard way) to strive for a balance between downtime, academics, and an activity or two.

Mistake #6:
Unreasonable Expectations

Most schools, whether public or private, offer some amount of heterogeneous groupings—a fancy phrase for ability-level grouping, usually offering below-average, average, or above-average classes. This may take the form of the "Sparrows," "Robins," or "Cardinals" for third grade reading groups, honors language arts class versus regular language arts in middle school, or advanced placement courses yielding college credits versus traditional classes in the high school setting. Teacher expectations vary considerably for kids in the "Cardinals," honors, or advanced placement classes as compared to their peers in the traditional groups. Gifted kids (generally testing with IQs of 130 or greater) tend to inhabit the advanced-level classes, whereas the traditional courses contain kids with a wide range of ability.

Although it would seem that placement in the higher-level courses would yield greater learning, that's not always what occurs. Theresa was a good example of this. A seventh grader with a terrific work ethic, Theresa was attending three honors courses (language arts, science, and math), along with three traditional ones (geography, physical education, and computer). Theresa studied constantly—her parents estimated between two and four hours each night. She rarely complained, but did become upset when she couldn't watch a favorite television show because a report was due the next day or she had to study on weekends just to keep up with the advanced curriculum. Theresa's folks had pushed for her placement in the advanced classes because her older brother, Sean, had sailed through the higher-level programs in both middle and high school, was a National Merit Finalist, and had obtained an academic scholarship to Penn State. Since Sean had been so successful, Theresa's folks expected the same of her. Both kids had strong study skills, were responsible, and rarely forgot to do their homework. The difference, though, was in their innate ability. Theresa was bright, but her brother was what I refer to as "spooky smart." You know, the type of kid who catches on to calculus and physics by just listening to the teacher's lecture and can whip out a great opinion paper the first time around sitting at the computer keyboard. Theresa's parents couldn't understand why she was struggling so—she paid attention in class, did all available extra credit, but seemed to miss an A in honors science and language arts by a few points each grading period. Theresa was frustrated and so were her parents, and her school guidance counselor referred them to me to figure out what the problem was.

After I interviewed Theresa, I was sure that it wasn't a study skill or motivational problem. This kid was trying *too hard* and it was beginning to damage her self-concept. If Sean could fly through these same courses with half the effort, she wondered what was wrong with her. I administered a battery of tests, including an IQ test and an achievement series. The results suggested that there was absolutely nothing wrong with Theresa—it was Sean who was different! Her IQ was above average and all scores on the achievement tests suggested that she was working in the above-average range, right where she should be. Theresa was on target academically, a bright kid who worked hard and was learning at an above-average pace. The problem was that Theresa's honors classes were geared to students with superior and very superior IQs—the top 10 percent of children her age. Like her brother, Sean, they caught on to concepts quickly and could finish about half of their homework during class. Theresa usually spent any free time she had in school getting extra help from the teachers and asking for concepts to be repeated if she hadn't understood them the first time around. To put it succinctly—Theresa was in over her head. Her terrific motivation helped as she eventually learned most of the concepts through tutoring or perseverance, but the toll that it was taking on her free time as well as on her self-concept just wasn't worth it.

It's tough to deal with a situation like this when describing ability levels to parents and their kids. I didn't want to discourage Theresa from reaching for the stars, but understanding reality also would be important to her. When I described to Theresa that she was an above-average kid, but not brilliant like her brother, Sean, I don't think that this came as a surprise to her. She'd been aware for many years that concepts came quickly to Sean, whereas she had to work at them. Theresa appreciated the information, I believe it let her off the hook in a fashion. We still expected good grades, since she was a smart kid, but she would have to chose between working diligently in honors classes to receive a B or to move down a level and make A's. Theresa's decision was to stick it out for the remainder of the school year in her current curriculum and to drop to a regular-language arts class for eighth grade. She loved science and math and committed to the honors curriculum, even though it would be tough at times. Theresa's folks handled this situation beautifully. They realized that their daughter had been under too much pressure and that being compared to her older brother was unfair. They vowed to treat her more as an individual and to back up her academic decisions, since they trusted her judgment.

It's important to know your child's relative strengths and weaknesses and to treat her as an individual. How you did in school when you were a kid or how other siblings fared is not always relevant. If your child is trying hard, yet struggling, in an honors program, take another look and perhaps get a second opinion about how appropriate the fit between the student and the curriculum is. Making the mistake of not treating each child on an individual basis can often lead to either expecting too much or too little from the youngster and can have a significant impact on their self-concept.

~~~~~~ Figure 2

Are You Sabotaging Your Child's Academic Success?

Are you on the wrong track when it comes to your expectations about your kid's academic behavior and responsibilities? Take this short quiz and see how you fare:

1. Will you give in to your kid's bugging and hassling and let him go outside to play, even though the rule is that homework must be completed first?

2. Do you despise confrontation and avoid it like the plague, placating your child, just so he won't whine and fuss?

3. Do you feel that your good tax dollars are paying the teachers' salaries and, therefore, *they* should be *totally responsible* for not only assigning homework but also making sure that your daughter gets it done?

4. Do you feel that it's always up to the teacher to contact you if a behavior or performance problem occurs in school and that "No news is good news"?

5. Do you believe that if your child is criticized then you are being criticized?

6. Is your kid perfect and whoever doesn't think so is either jealous or flat-out wrong?

7. Does your son have the uncanny ability of starting his homework each night, yet you consistently end up finishing it for him?

8. Does your kid go to school unprepared because he never quite understood the homework concepts as you gave him the answers?

9. Do you feel that a well-rounded kid is a "Jack of all trades" and should be exposed to all age-appropriate activities, even though her homework suffers?

10. Does "clearing the table" mean throwing away wrappers and fast-food bags in the trash four or five

nights a week as you drive through for dinner, in between extracurricular activities with little time left for studying?

11. Are you outwardly proud of one child's accomplishments yet disappointed that the other is "just average," even though she seems to be trying her best in school?

12. Were you a math whiz and expect the same from your son, who can't seem to remember his multiplication tables from one day to the next, yet writes like John Grisham? Do you focus on his math deficits and ignore his creative writing strengths?

If you've answered *yes* to at least six of the above items, then most likely you're actually interfering with your child's success in school. Check out the next chapter, "*The Benevolent Dictator,*" to help get you back on track and to be a more effective parent.

four

The Benevolent Dictator

~~~~~~

The previous chapter described specific mistakes parents make in dealing with their children's academic difficulties. To maximize parental effectiveness, not only in terms of academic achievement but also in other areas of child responsibility, parents often seek a style of parenting that is comfortable, natural, and effective. Running a family is analogous in many ways to running a country. There's a budget to decide upon, wars to put out, laws to make, and a hierarchy of decision-makers to deal with. Just as in the political arena, families can be run on a continuum from democracy to dictatorship to autocracy, with great variance in between.

There is no one best method by which to run a family—a lot depends upon the tolerance level of the parents and the personalities and habits of individual family members. If the children are reasonable and self-motivated, then a democratic style of parenting may be effective, with all members having an equal vote and therefore a similar voice in decision-making. Choosing the summer vacation spot can be a compromise between Mom and Dad's desire to relax and the kids' need for plenty of running room and neat experiences—a trip to the beach may do the trick!

But what if the kids are less than reasonable, tending to put their own needs and desires before others? Can a democracy work? Probably not, but most families usually give it a whirl at first. Endless hours of arguing and listening to "But that's not fair . . . we always have to do what my sister wants" ensue. When kids have difficulty seeing things from others' perspectives, the democratic process breaks down and everyone gets sent to their rooms. More often than not a failed family democracy swings 180 degrees to a strict autocracy, with the kids feeling as if their vote doesn't count at all to their frazzled parents.

That's where running the family as a *benevolent dictatorship* comes in. *Benevolent dictator* parents listen to their children, consider their desires, yet retain final voting and vetoing rights for themselves. John Rosemond in *Parent Power! A Common-Sense Approach to Parenting in the '90s and Beyond* promotes *benevolent dictators* as those who do not "demand unquestioning obedience. They encourage questions, but make the final decision. They restrict their children's freedom, but they are not tyrants. They restrict in order to protect and guide . . . Life with a *benevolent dictator* is predictable and secure for children." This teaches the child self-control and frustration tolerance, which we have seen in the previous chapters to be paramount in promoting academic achievement.

Becoming a Benevolent Dictator

There is an art to becoming a *benevolent dictator*, though. To many of us, it is an unnatural style—we may not like to be the decision-maker, or perhaps we're touchy about saying no to our kids, or we'll do anything just to get the child off our back to stop the bugging and hassling! It definitely takes some backbone to make the deciding vote, especially if it's unpopular with the troops. Often when I'm working with parents new to my practice, we first spend time on general behavior management parenting techniques before focusing specifically on the child's academic problems. Remember Candice—the *if-then student* from Chapter Two? I had to teach her folks to give effective consequences depending upon whether or not she completed her work that day. In doing so, her parents needed to feel comfortable with the *behavior/consequence connection*—that kids receive rewards for appropriate behaviors and punishments for inappropriate actions.

It's amazing how many folks dislike this part of parenting! Most enjoy handing out the rewards, but few relish the punishments. The reasons vary from not wanting to disappoint the kid by removing a privilege to not having the time at night to put the child in time-out. No one has said that parenting is a picnic, it's not, but you usually reap what you sow. The "sowing" gets old at times, especially when you're dealing with a bullheaded, *if-then student* or a cunning, *manipulative student.* Throw into the mixture the reality that in most families both Mom and Dad work all day, and as Dr. T. Berry Brazelton notes in his book *Touchpoints: Your Child's Emotional and Behavioral Development,* "When both parents are away at work all day, they hate to be disciplinarians in their little time at home." These folks often prefer to ignore poor child behavior or failure to complete homework, just to get through the evening in one piece.

Mary Pipher, a delightful, level-headed psychologist and author of *Reviving Ophelia: Saving the Souls of Adolescent Girls,* also bemoans the laissez-faire attitudes that many parents take. She talks of a mother who confused *parenting* with *abuse:* "The mother was trying so hard to be good to her daughter that she was denying her the chance to grow up." Pipher felt that the mother was in danger of "understanding her daughter all the way into juvenile court." In other words, it's important to listen to your kids' desires, but when they become unreasonable, it's time to pull out the *benevolent dictator* role and cast the final vote.

Junior may have a dozen excuses for not doing his homework, but in the long run your vote is the one that matters and he should receive a negative consequence if he doesn't comply. Decades of psychological research overwhelmingly show that actions speak louder than words. Trying to talk a fourth grader into making better grades, reasoning with him, and explaining the results of poor study skills on college admission can be like banging your head against the wall. Reasoning with the unreasonable just doesn't work! When the horse is dead, it's time to get off and try a new tactic. If you're still treating homework completion as the child's choice and it's not getting done, then he's probably too immature to use good judgment and you may have to make homework decisions for him until common sense finally kicks in.

As a *benevolent dictator*, you have permission to parent again. Somewhere in the past few decades psychologists, talk-show experts, pediatricians, and even teachers have strayed from the good old-fashioned discipline that kept many of us in line as kids. Now, I'm not suggesting using physical consequences, such as spankings or swattings—when I refer to discipline, I mean creating the *behavior/consequence connection* for the child. This teaches kids that they are responsible for their actions as well as promoting self-discipline and teaching good frustration tolerance. So many of the kids I see today as miserable, depressed, grumpy, whiney, or bratty are really just lacking in self-discipline—they can't take no for an answer and will drive their folks nuts until Mom or Dad caves in and says yes.

The *benevolent dictator* has the guts not to fall into this trap. Because he is benevolent, Dad will listen to the plaintiff's arguments and try to negotiate a solution. But if the child is not accepting of the plea agreement—Dad makes the final judgment and any grumping and complaining can be taken to the bedroom. Although at the moment Dad may feel guilty for upsetting his sixth grader by insisting that homework be completed before shooting hoops, it sure beats the guilt associated with watching the kid drop out of school years later as a teenager.

I'm convinced (by my own clinical experience, as well as the research literature) that kids are more content growing up in a household with clear guidelines and limits. Although few will ask for curfews to be imposed, most respect the security of knowing exactly what the parental expectations are. It's in households where the rules are *consistently inconsistent* that concern me—kids either roll the dice and hope that Mom is distracted and will overlook the teacher's negative note, or they are so uncertain of Dad's moods that they become chronically anxious—anticipating the worst even if they've been good that day. Both outcomes lead to academic underachievement—kids who inconsistently study for tests or skip homework assignments are not prepared for class and the chronically anxious child often is too distracted to focus upon learning.

The *benevolent dictator* parent is consistent—the established rules stand for today as well as for next week or month. Homework before play, maintaining a minimum GPA to keep the car keys, and respectful behavior determine privileges and curfews. When kids can count on consistent rules and therefore consistent parental reactions, they feel that they have some control over their world. That's extremely important to emotional growth and the development of good self-esteem. There's security in being the master of one's fate—it's fair, reasonable, and kids just like it. That's why the *benevolent dictator* role proves to be so successful in parenting all kinds of kids. The *if-then student* responds beautifully to the clear rules, as do *chameleon*, *manipulative*, and *disorganized students*. Even reasonable, self-motivated students are not put off by the guidelines set, as long as they are fair (remember, benevolent means kind!).

But what if you had difficulty learning self-control yourself as a kid and are just getting the hang of it now as an adult? Sure—it will be a challenge to set rules and to be consistent with your own children. Instead of dwelling upon your early behaviors of skipping classes, copying others' homework, or not even bothering to turn in any homework at all, focus upon the price that irresponsibility has probably cost you over the years. Although you may have landed on your feet after several false starts, life most likely would have been easier if you had not taken the easy way out in your earlier years. Becoming a parent has a way of making one grow up quickly, like it or not. When you're responsible not only for your own actions, but also for those of your child's, you tend to think twice before reacting impulsively and skipping work, having one too many drinks, or telling off the boss in anger.

Although it may not be in your nature to set consistent rules, reviewing the price you may have paid as a kid and young adult just may motivate you to become a *benevolent dictator* in order to help your child avoid the same consequences. Many clients tell me that since it's not in their nature to be consistent with or able to confront their kids, that it's unreasonable for me to expect them to change. The bottom line is that it's *unreasonable for them not to change* bad habits, such as making the *peace at any price* mistake or being uninvolved with their kid's education, as are *leave it to the teacher* parents. The buck has to stop at some point and blaming the teacher, the school system, or your ex-spouse are just excuses—not solutions.

There are no good reasons for lack of involvement with your child's education, only lame cop-outs. I've worked with stressed-out, overworked, financially strapped single parents who care enough to learn how to be terrific *benevolent dictators*. These folks ignore the obstacles and take the bull by the horns, they set up good communication with the school, give clear guidelines to the kids, and administer consistent and fair consequences. No amount of hand-wringing or whining can compete with the effect that this style of parenting has on your child's ultimate academic achievement. And remember, you are your child's first and foremost teacher. If she sees you learning self-control, tolerating frustration by skipping your favorite television show in order to quiz her for her science test, she'll develop this type of self-discipline naturally. Whether we like it or not, our kids are watching us like hawks and inculcating many of our values as their own. Not only does your daughter get her blue eyes from you, but her work ethic will ultimately be colored by how responsibly you behave, the degree of your commitment to her education, and the self-discipline you show. As Dr. M. Scott Peck so eloquently notes in *The Road Less Traveled: A New Psychology of Love, Traditional Values, and Spiritual Growth*: "Discipline is the basic set of tasks we require to solve life's problems. Without discipline we can solve nothing, and with some discipline we can solve only some problems. With total discipline we can solve all problems." Is the *benevolent dictator* style of parenting beginning to sound enticing? I hope so because it encourages parents to parent—to guide, to set limits, and to establish expectations that lead kids to realizing their academic potential.

But I Don't Want to
Call the Shots . . .

Vicki was having a tough time coming to terms with the *benevolent dictator* concept. As a single parent since Kristin was two years old, she was trying to raise her daughter as a friend, a buddy, and at times a confidante. As a preschooler, Kristin was generally compliant and even when she did become ornery, Vicki could either talk her into seeing things her way, manipulate the situation to dispel the temper tantrum, or just leave the mall and take the fussy kid home. Things worked out—not always smoothly, but if misbehavior ended an evening early, it was no big deal.

Kristin got out of hand, though, when she entered grade school and began to be sassy with not only her mother, but her teachers as well. Vicki put up with it through grade school, but in middle school Kristin began to sneak out at night, to lie about her homework, and to be disrespectful to her teachers at school. Lecturing, reasoning, and threatening had little effect upon this preteen and Vicki was frightened that she was losing control of her daughter. Treating her as a buddy only worked when there was something in it for Kristin (going shopping at the mall) and trying to reason with her often resulted in arguments and back talk.

Vicki was attending a women's therapy group run by my associate, who referred her to me after seeing how frustrated this single mom was. Vicki described her parenting style as democratic—giving Kristin an equal vote and at times the only vote. It just hadn't been worth standing up to the kid through the years and Vicki usually ended up taking the easy way out and giving in. But the little girl had grown into a willful, unreasonable young lady who abused her mother's good nature. Vicki had become so frustrated with Kristin's shenanigans that lately she had reversed her tactics—instead of giving her daughter the benefit of the doubt, she now tended to not even listen to Kristin's argument, assuming that she was being manipulative, sneaky, or was trying to con her mother into something. Their relationship had deteriorated so much that Vicki smacked her daughter on the cheek when Kristin brought home another poor report card and tried to make excuses for the failing grades. Vicki had never hit her daughter before and this not only startled Kristin, but forced her mom into realizing that her democratic style of parenting wasn't going to work with this kid. Kristin's feelings seemed to sting more than did her face and she described resentment and anger to me when I asked her about the incident. Admitting to being a handful—rude, disrespectful, and unmotivated, she'd never suspected that her mother would lose it. Mom had always put up with her misbehavior before and even seemed to give in the louder she complained or fussed. Apparently the last report card, coupled with Vicki's growing feelings of inadequacy as a parent, had pushed her mother over the line—from trying to be a democratic parent to parenting as an unfair autocrat.

When I saw both of them together in my office, I described what had occurred over the years—how Vicki had taken the easy way out as a parent—placating her daughter, putting out emotional fires as they occurred, but never seeming to stick with a game plan for setting limits, guidelines, and consequences. Kristin, at twelve years of age, now felt that the rug was being pulled out from under her, the rules had abruptly been changed without her permission or even a vote, and she was beginning to feel alienated from her mom. Although she admitted that she'd regularly taken advantage of Vicki, she felt that she had been allowed to, even encouraged to, because there rarely was a punishment for misbehaving and most of the time her fussing had led to getting what she wanted. Vicki's reaction to a failed democracy was to establish an instant autocracy—with Mom holding total power and Kristin feeling as if she had no control at all. Obviously, neither mother nor daughter felt comfortable with the new arrangement—it was not well thought out but was more of a knee-jerk reaction to Vicki's growing intolerance with her demanding daughter. I suggested that we try setting up a *benevolent dictatorship* and described to each what roles and responsibilities they would have. Rules about home life (chores and shared responsibilities), academics (work and behavior in school), and mutual respect would have to be developed. Vicki's expectations needed to be spelled out, as well as consequences developed (both positive and negative) for appropriate and inappropriate behavior. And finally the family would need to stick with the guidelines that they established—no coping out, giving in, or changing rules in midstream just to avoid a confrontation.

Kristin would have a voice in the decision-making, but Vicki would have the final vote. I suggested that at times their desires would be the same, sometimes they would agree to disagree, and at other times Kristin would have to give in and follow the rules, even if she didn't like them.

The outcome would be that Vicki would feel that she had the right to parent, even if her decisions were at times unpopular. Kristin would be able to predict the consequences of her actions and to choose her behavior accordingly. It would be more fair than before, both when Kristin was running the show as well as when Vicki lost it and became an unfair autocrat, not listening to her daughter and smacking her due to frustration.

The *benevolent dictator* parenting style certainly was foreign to Vicki's nature, but she was able to adapt to it. She realized that Kristin's adolescence was quickly approaching and they would be experiencing lots of predictable bumps in the road as well as unplanned emergencies. To survive this in one piece, both mother and daughter needed a behavioral program that was structured, fair, and clear to all. It's easier to be a parent, as well as a kid, when life is predictable—and that's just what the *benevolent dictatorship* brought into their lives.

five

Teaching Your Kids
the Behavior/Consequence
Connection

~~~~~~

One of the major development hurdles that all kids must master is understanding and accepting the *behavior/consequence connection*. Even little ones are quick studies at this: "If I throw the spoon down on the floor, Dad picks it up" or "If I cry long and loud enough, Mom will come get me." As children grow older and their ability to conceptualize becomes more sophisticated, the connection between their behavior and the consequences that they receive becomes evident. "If I hit on the playground, most likely I'll get hit back" or "If I do what Mom says, she'll praise me, or at the very least she'll stop nagging me."

Kids make thousands of these connections by the time they enter kindergarten—they quickly learn the politics of making and breaking friendships, angering or pleasing their parents, and the behaviors needed to maintain or to de-crease in order to get what they want or to avoid unpleas-ant circumstances. This association involves making the *behavior/consequence connection*, a process that is governed by the environment—taught by the significant people in your child's life, his parents, child care workers, peers, siblings, and teachers. First, the child needs to *learn* what behaviors produce what consequences. As noted above, this is not a difficult process, one which tends to occur naturally over time as the youngster interacts with significant others. The second step—that of *accepting* the *behavior/consequence connection* is more difficult for many kids, even for some adults. Many feel that they are above the rules and that the con-nection shouldn't pertain to them, whereas others may feel that all rules are unfair unless they are self-imposed. Kids who have trouble accepting the connection are often later found in school dropout prevention programs or juvenile detention centers, and adults who rebel against this con-cept never quite seem to make it in our society. The *behavior/consequence connection* is a major key to success in life—be it within the family, socially with friends, or suc-ceeding academically and vocationally. Because of the im-portance of making the connection, it is at the core of ef-fective parenting and an important base for understanding child behavior management guidelines.

Let's take a close look at the *behavior/consequence connec-tion*—why it works and how you can effectively teach your child this association. First, consider the concept of conse-quences. Most folks simply view them as rewards or pun-ishments. When polled, many parents report using time-out, loss of privileges, going to bed early, or loss of the car keys for older kids. For many children these consequences are effective, but for others they may not work because they are not used in an effective manner. For instance, putting a seven-year-old in time-out for seven minutes usually won't make an impression upon him—by the time the kid realizes that he's being punished in his bedroom, it's almost time to leave. However, twenty minutes would probably get his attention and a time-out spot other than his bedroom (which is often a playtime free-for-all) helps speed up the process. *Consequences must be perceived by the child as being either significantly pleasant or significantly unpleasant in order to get the kid's attention and the desired behavioral effect.*

Pleasurable consequences should feel good (a back rub, an "atta boy"), taste good (candy, driving through McDonald's for fries and a Coke), look good (credit earned toward a new shirt or bathing suit), or be fun (use of video games, television, telephone, going to an arcade, or having a sleepover). Unpleasant consequences need to hurt—not in the physical sense as would a spanking, but they must bother the child in other ways. Time-out, loss of privilege, and being sent to bed early can be effective if these actions are perceived as significantly unpleasant to the child.

The question to be asked is: "Will this *particular consequence* (either positive or negative) be meaningful to this *particular kid?*" Not only do you need to take into account the nature of the consequence (perhaps time-out), but how long it will be in effect (ten minutes, an hour, three hours), and where it will occur (the child's bedroom, a hall corner, or in a safe bathroom). Just about any consequence can be made more meaningful if given in an effective manner (considering length of time and setting) rather than haphazardly administering it.

In addition to timing and setting, parental consistency when meting out consequences is extremely important. Most kids I see report that Mom and Dad are big on threats: "Go to your room . . . forever," "You're losing the car . . . forever," "No more television . . . forever," but rarely follow through. Who could stick with anything *forever*? It makes more sense to threaten a consequence that's easy to follow through with (both emotionally and physically), such as loss of television privileges for three or four days, than to figure out how to keep your child from watching TV for an extended period of time. Also, parents tend to feel less guilty when giving out more reasonable consequences, they have fewer regrets and therefore they tend to stick with it. Mom most likely will be able to take away the television for twenty-four hours—it's no picnic listening to Junior's gripes, but it's doable. So before issuing a consequence statement (whether it's a positive or negative one), stop and think—are you really up for making sure that Junior has no television for a year or would a week be more realistic? Are you really going to buy the kid a pony if she makes the honor roll next grading period or would it be smarter to promise some horseback riding lessons? In a pinch, I find it best that when there needs to be a consequence and you're not sure what to do, announce it later in the day after you've had time to calmly think about what's going to have the best chance of success—both in terms of follow-through, as well as the effect it will have upon the child. Be smart, count to ten, take a walk around the block—it's better to hold off and discuss the consequence later than to have to go back on your word and look inconsistent to your child.

No matter how good you get at giving consequences, though, there's always the stinker who's a pro at wearing you down. Ren was such a character, his parents had set up the very clear rule that his weekend privileges depended totally upon the Friday report from school. If it was acceptable then this thirteen-year-old could have a sleepover, go to the movies, and pretty much hang out on the weekends, which is what he wanted to do. The *behavior* (a good Friday school report)/*consequence* (free weekend) rule was clear—no ifs, ands, or buts about it. Yet week after week Ren would come home with some sort of twist to the report card. One Friday he said that he'd lost it but that his mother could call all of his teachers if she wanted to. Another week only four of the six teachers had filled out and signed off on it (Ren said that there was an assembly that day, but he had no way of proving it), and yet on another Friday one teacher's signature looked awfully fishy to his folks.

Facing the loss of a good weekend (basically being grounded from leaving the home or watching TV), Ren would make valiant attempts at convincing his parents to give in—and they usually did. It's difficult to stand up to a kid who keeps bugging, hassling, demanding, and accusing his parents of being unfair. Most of us would cave in, just to get the kid out of our hair. And trust me, the child not only knows that this will occur, but is actually counting on it! Ren knew that he could wear his mother down easier than his father, so he would begin his frontal attack with her, accomplish his mission, and then hit his father up. Knowing that Dad didn't want to start the weekend off on a bad footing by arguing with Mom, he accurately predicted that Dad would acquiesce and go along with Mom's letting Ren get away with it. This kid was no dummy—if only he would put half the thought into completing his school-work!

Consequences work in changing kids' behavior, but only when they are either significantly pleasant or signifi-cantly unpleasant to the child. Lukewarm doesn't cut it. Rewards need to feel good and punishments should be un-pleasant. The time, setting and nature of the consequence should be tailored to the individual child, not necessarily taken from what works for the kid next door. I once worked with a child who wanted figs for completing his homework on time. Why figs? I don't know but it really didn't matter! If figs were pleasurable and important enough to motivate learning multiplication facts, then figs it would be!

Also, consider meting out consequences in a *nonchalant manner*. A screaming parent doing a meltdown can be quite amusing to a cagey kid. Sure, no one wants to see their folks mad, but Mom sure looks funny when she throws her hands up in the air with that totally exasperated look! Some children actually get off on this—driving their folks nuts gives them a feeling of control over their parents' emotions, which power-hungry, tyrannical children seem to enjoy. So, if Junior doesn't get his work done on time, take away the figs in a calm, nonchalant manner—it's not necessary to throw them against a wall while stomping out of the room! Do whatever it takes to stay calm (count to ten, take a short walk around the block, complain to your spouse) and then give the consequence—calmly and firmly. Next, make sure that the rules governing the *behavior/consequence connection* are clear and fair. If homework is to be done before play, then this should *always* be the rule—not just on days when you're paying attention and not distracted by your own chores or telephone calls to return. Make it clear what completing homework means. For instance, all worksheets need to be finished accurately, handwriting is reasonably neat, and the bookbag should be packed for the next day. If the child is to study for a quiz or test, try to clarify what "studying" actually means. To some kids it means as little as bringing the book home, whereas to others it means memorizing the material. It's best to expect conceptual understanding—that not only is the work reviewed (book chapter, class notes, worksheets), but a short quiz given at home to help the child realize what he does and doesn't understand. Many children do not realize what they don't know—therefore they feel that they know it all and further study is just not necessary! Once your son realizes that he's got the dates down pat for the battles of the 1800s, but doesn't remember the catalysts that set off the wars, he'll be able to concentrate on the weak areas of his knowledge by going back and gaining understanding of that time period, and probably doing well on the test.

I've found it to be extremely helpful in clarifying expectations to use a calendar system for long-term projects and a countdown timer for daily assignments. Long-term projects, such as a book report, can be broken down into the number of pages to be read each day, as well as the dates that the rough draft and final draft are to be completed. These should be marked on a homework calendar that is checked and completed every day (even weekends as it may be necessary to perform Saturday work for long-range assignments). Countdown timers are terrific tools for clarifying how long each daily assignment should take—twenty minutes for ten math problems, thirty minutes for vocabulary sentences. These procedures work well for children who tend to procrastinate beginning a task as well as for those who lose motivation and begin to dawdle midtask. Timing makes it clear and fair as to what is expected and the child has the choice as to whether he'll beat the buzzer and receive a pleasurable consequence or to slack off and receive an unpleasant one.

Also, be sure that the consequence portion of the *behavior* (studying)/*consequence* (reward or punishment) *connection* is clear. Does "No TV until all the work is completed" also mean no video games or video tapes? Does it include not watching television at the neighbor's house? Try to think of as many of the possible cracks that your child can slip through—if you don't think of them, you can bet that he's going to and will have no qualms about hitting you up with "Well, you didn't say I couldn't watch TV at 12:01 A.M., you just said no TV tonight and I held off until early this morning . . . I didn't break the rule!" Many times we find ourselves trying to reason with the unreasonable, so don't be too upset with this type of convoluted logic. It's just a normal kid trying to get around the rule, but if you keep the *behavior/consequence connection* clear, it's tough for the child to manipulate or sabotage the system.

Finally, try to make the *behavior/consequence connection* fair. Let your kid have a voice as to what appropriate studying (the behavior) really means, as well as what the consequence should be (no television anywhere for twenty-four hours, going to bed early for not completing the task, or receiving a daily allowance for a job well done.) Remember, though, that *benevolent dictator* parents encourage the child to have a say in the decision-making process, but the final vote comes from Mom or Dad.

Now that we've reviewed how to give consequences effectively, let's discuss the various types that seem to work best for each age group. The flow chart on page 102 delineates both positive and negative consequences available for use by parents trying to motivate good kid academic achievement.

Positive Consequences

Positive consequences (rewards) tend to fall within three categories—activities, affirmations, and material reinforcers. Some kids enjoy all three areas, whereas others like to focus upon only one or two. Your child's individual nature will help determine which ones you should use in your home.

Activity Rewards

Let's say that your eleven-year-old son actually completes his homework on Friday night rather than employing his usual tactic of leaving it until Sunday evening. Once you've picked yourself up from the floor and can think clearly

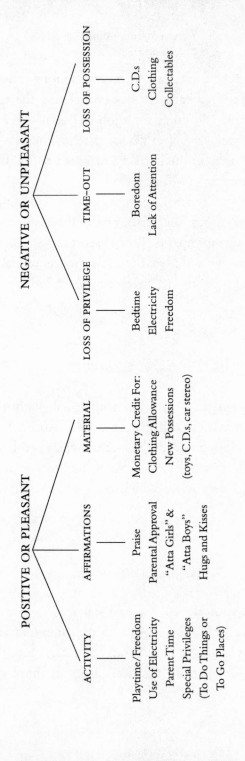

Figure 3
Consequences

again, you decide that an activity reward is in order. You announce that he'll be allowed that weekend to stay up late on Friday night and to have a friend sleep over on Saturday. Most likely your kid will think something to the effect of "Hey, since I've completed my homework on Friday, Mom and Dad are letting me stay up late tonight and have a friend stay over on Saturday. That's pretty cool—maybe I should do this more often!"

Psychologists have long known that rewarded behavior tends to continue and your son will most likely learn to tone down his procrastination in order to again receive the positive consequence of a fun weekend. But if being allowed to have someone sleep over is no big deal to your child, it probably will not motivate him to get his act together and complete his work early. Remember, when using activity rewards, they must be important, enticing, and pleasurable to the individual child.

The activity rewards enjoyed by children differ by age and stage of development as well as upon individual personality characteristics, likes and dislikes of your kid. Keep this in mind when reviewing the following list of possible activity reinforcers.

Grade-schoolers

➤ **Playtime/Freedom:** Grade-schoolers enjoy permission to go outside and play or to have a friend over. They love roller blading, bike riding, shooting hoops, swimming, and playing board games. Movement and fun is what this category is all about.

➤ **Use of Electricity:** This involves permission to use anything that either plugs into the wall or necessitates batteries. (Note: I never take away lights, blow dryers, or alarm clocks!) Electricity consists of, but is not limited to, television, video games, video tapes, telephone, computer, remote control cars, handheld video games, radio, stereo, CD player, and walkie-talkies. I may have missed some that your individual child uses, so be creative—your kid may be addicted to listening to the police frequency band, that uses electricity too and therefore falls into this category! Activity rewards work because kids *hate to be bored* and *love to be amused*. Grade school electricity use generally centers around watching television, playing video games as well as watching video tapes. These kids are not yet living on the telephone and many are not yet hooked on music, so the radio and CD player may not be as important as are television and video games and tapes.

➤ **Parent Time:** Grade-schoolers still like their folks. They will walk with you at the mall and still claim that you're their mom or dad. They love to play—either outside shooting hoops or involved in a quick game of flag football or riding bikes together. These kids enjoy showing off new skills and having you watch their thirty-third attempt at performing a cartwheel. They also enjoy playing board games, watching a favorite video together, or taking a walk with a parent. This is a nice time of life—when the kid actually likes and needs you, you're still important and activities together are treasured. Now, I'm not suggesting that the only time that you play with your grade-schooler is as a reward for appropriate behavior—those times may be too few and far between! I am proposing, though, to be careful to *not* play a board game with your daughter on an evening when she's left her books at school and therefore can't complete her homework. And be sure to announce on the good school days that she gets to pick the parent activity you do together *because* she's been responsible and completed her work in a timely manner.

➤ **Special Privileges:** (to go places or to engage in extra activities): If polled, most folks feel like chauffeurs just driving their children to the necessary activities such as school, lessons, and sports events. On top of that many grade-schoolers beg to be taken to the park, to play with friends from their old neighborhood (at least a twenty-minute drive each way), to go to the arcade, or to have a sleepover. I consider these activities to be privileges, to be earned rather than received just because they bugged you about it. Grade-schoolers can earn these activity rewards by showing good study skills and habits throughout the week and can "cash in" and receive a special privilege activity on the weekend.

Middle-schoolers

➤ **Play Time/Freedom:** As kids grow, so does the list of desired activity rewards. Play time not only involves having friends over but children like the freedom of walking to others' homes or to the local convenience store. Biking, roller blading, and shooting hoops are still important, but middle-schoolers are beginning to push for extended freedoms.

➤ **Electricity:** Electricity takes on a new dimension with middle-schoolers—the telephone, Internet chatting with buddies, or playing computer games on the net become lifelines for your kids. Music also grows in importance. It seems like the child can't do anything without a CD playing or the radio blasting. Television and video games remain high on their list of desired activities, as does watching video tapes.

➤ **Parent Time:** During the middle school years, the "coolness factor" begins to kick in. Although your daughter may actually still like you, she's probably beginning to be cautious about showing this in public. At home, she's still a kid and enjoys taking walks, goofing around, and spending time together. At this age parent time activity rewards include going out to lunch together, checking out the puppies at the SPCA, fishing from the pier, and playing board games together.

➤ **Special Privileges:** Most preteens and early teenagers love to spend nights at friends' houses or to have a buddy sleep over at their own home. Throw in some pizza and a video and it's a night to be remembered! Middle-schoolers enjoy going to arcades, walking the mall with a friend, or checking out the latest laser tag or aggressive skate park.

High Schoolers

Teenagers are a breed unto themselves. Whoever said that high school was the best time of life needs to get a life! It's often a chaotic, painful, lonely, wild, exciting existence—

definitely not boring and often very stressful. The teenage years are the middle ground between childhood and becoming an adult, and the back and forth swings between the two often drive parents (as well as their kids) nuts! The child who just yesterday successfully navigated downtown traffic to pick up Grandma at the airport today cannot seem to remember where the trash cans are supposed to go. Or your sixteen-year-old daughter barely waves to you at the mall when she's walking with her friends, but still demands her bedtime back rubs and talks in private. These seeming incongruities and mood swings are normal—at times acting too grown up juxtaposed with reverting to the little kid you remember. (What's even more weird is when they do it within the same day!) These behaviors are logical, if you consider the forces acting upon the teenager. It's hard to give up the fun things they enjoyed as a child or preteen (doing cannonballs in the pool and splashing their parents or playing capture the flag in the backyard). But these are definitely uncool activities in front of their friends. The quest for freedom and independence is very strong—now that Junior has the car keys, the boundaries seem endless. When each of my kids first started driving, they'd use every excuse to take the car: "Gotta have a Slurpee from the Quickie Mart or I can't get to sleep" or "I need a new pencil, guess I'll just have to go to Target and check out their supply." They used to be able to handle drinking whatever was in the refrigerator or scrounging up a pencil, but the call of freedom (taking the car) was just too strong. Any excuse to hit the road, to feel the independence of going places when they wanted to, not when Mom or Dad finally got around to it, was overwhelming.

Because of teens' needs for independence and new experiences, activity rewards can be tremendously effective in motivating them to achieve in school. They may not like to admit it, but better grades confirm the effectiveness of the following reinforcers:

➤ **Playtime/Freedom:** Teens want to go places—enjoying biking, roller blading, and exploring. Of course, car privileges are treasured and most kids will complete homework if there's wheels in it for them!

➤ **Use of Electricity:** Like middle-schoolers, many high schoolers live for the telephone, television, video games, computer time, and their favorite music. They seem to be lost without the ability to communicate with friends (on the phone or on chat lines) and swear that they cannot study without their music playing in the background. Not being able to see their favorite talk show, sitcom, or series on television ("But, Dad, tonight's episode is the *most* important of the whole year . . . *everyone* will be watching it!") really hurts, and kids will work to not lose this privilege.

➤ **Parent Time:** Teens spending time with their folks is somewhat of a dichotomy—almost totally forbidden in public unless it's the only way to get to the ball game or to the concert, or to con Mom into buying some new outfits. At home, they still like to communicate and fool around with their folks, but most teens I know will not work for parent time as a reward. Some even consider it to be a punishment! Obviously this activity becomes less rewarding for the older crowd than for grade-schoolers, who actually treasure playing a board game with their folks. (Not to worry, though, soon they'll be adults, married with kids of their own who will ignore them and you'll feel vindicated!)

➤ **Special Privileges:** Permission to attend special events is very enticing to most teens. Going to concerts, parties, amusement parks, out to dinner, the movies, and having massive sleepovers are very enticing and can be used to effectively motivate good academic performance. And the value of all of these activities is greatly heightened if the kid can do it without his parents tagging along!

Affirmations

Affirmations are positive statements, either told to oneself or to another, as well as shows of affection. In general, kids love affirmations. These take the form of praise, parental approval ("atta girl" or "atta boy"), and especially hugs and kisses. Although some children won't admit to liking praise, kids love being told that they're doing a great job, are loved, or that you're really impressed with their new, great idea.

The types of affirmations enjoyed by children tend to vary by age and stage of development. Let's take a look at what seems to work by age group:

Grade-schoolers

Little kids love being praised for a job well done. "Wow, I couldn't have built that model when I was your age . . .

you're terrific with your hands!" is an affirmation worth its weight in gold. Just imagine how your child would feel after hearing that one! Or how about: "Boy, you did your math problems in record time, and they're all correct, I'm really impressed!" Add to this list:

- I'm proud of you!

- You're terrific!

- That was a responsible way to handle the situation!

- You really planned ahead . . . now you can take the weekend off because your book report is ready to be turned in on Monday.

- Look at these grades . . . none went down and your science grade went from a C to a B—good work!

- What a smart kid—you must have gotten your brains from my side of the family!

Many grade-schoolers also still love to be touched. Hugs, kisses, or a good-natured noogie to the head are usually well appreciated. Also, bragging to Grandma and Grandpa within your child's earshot spreads the good word and increases your child's self-esteem.

Middle-schoolers

Preteens and young teens still enjoy praise and compliments, but you've got to be sensitive to public shows of affection. An "atta boy" usually works, as might a "Good job . . . I'm proud of you. I know how hard you had to work at math this grading period!" However, the hugs and kisses may have to be saved for private moments, or your son and daughter may not appreciate them at all. During this stage of development, the most my son would tolerate was a kiss on the top of the head—and that was on a good day! Even though you may want to grab up the kid and give him a bear hug, try to respect his comfort zone—it's not rewarding to him if your show of affection violates his "area" and if it does, your well-intentioned hug may be perceived as an irritant.

Bragging to friends, neighbors, and relatives may also have to be toned down, as some middle-schoolers are beginning to think of getting good grades as "nerdy." You know your kid—if she enjoys a call to Grandma, then do it, but if she wants to keep her good grades to herself, then telling the neighbors may be off limits.

High Schoolers

The best way to deal with teens is to ask them directly how they would like you to handle their good grades. Most will be quite direct, telling you to praise them daily for at least a week or two and to display the good report card on the refrigerator, whereas others think it's definitely uncool to mention making the Dean's List. Respect her wishes, she knows that you're proud.

Teens also have very specific ideas about how their grades should be broadcast—some can't wait to brag to their cousins, whereas others are nonchalant and feel that their good grades are personal and shouldn't be discussed. Usually a hug or a noogie to the head does the trick when it comes to teens and physical praise. But some kids want more and others less. Again, your own child sets the tone and you should respect the limits that she desires. Remember—most kids enjoy verbal praise and affirmations, but may not tell you that they like them. As long as he does not recoil when you give an "atta boy," I'd continue to use this reward unless the kid makes it clear that it's uncomfortable to him. Even though it may feel strange to not be able to express your positive feelings as you'd like to, remember that your child is developing his own comfort zone and is checking out the limits within which he feels best.

Material Rewards

When thinking about rewarding children, most people automatically consider material reinforcers first—giving money or prizes for a job well done. But as we have just seen, activity rewards and affirmations can be very powerful reinforcers to kids of all ages. Material (tangible) rewards are important options to use because they are often easy to give, convenient, and important to the child. The use of material rewards, however, often divides parents into two theoretical camps—those who feel that giving kids money, clothing, or toys just for doing what they are supposed to do is wrong versus those who feel comfortable rewarding kids for making the extra effort. My philosophy is that in many families kids receive material rewards just for showing up alive on Saturday (receiving their weekly allowance) or are given a new outfit to wear just because it was on sale and too good a buy to pass up. Or Mom caved in and bought the new CD just to stop the kid's nagging. Personally, I'd rather have the child *earn* material rewards via a good school effort rather than be rewarded because it's Saturday or he's a pro at hassling his father. When I discuss use of material rewards with my clients and we figure out how much credit can be earned daily or weekly, most families find that it's actually cheaper to have kids earn their clothing, movie money, toy money, and so forth, than the haphazard system they've been using in the past (usually caving in to the kid's demands). Go for it—try adding material rewards to your list of reinforcers for good academic performance. You're spending the bucks anyway, so you might as well get something for your money! And don't worry that your child will need a new CD for every decent grade she gets in college—the power of good academic self-esteem will have taken over by then and she'll be making the grades for herself, not just to wrangle some goodies out of you!

The effectiveness of material rewards varies by age and stage of the child's development, as do activity rewards and affirmations. Little kids can be given inexpensive treats, whereas older children work best receiving credit toward larger items. Let's take a look at the hit list of some possible material rewards by age:

Grade-schoolers

Kindergarten and first graders usually enjoy receiving treats such as stickers, hand stamps, a colored marker with an activity book page, trading cards, play bracelets, toy cars, five pieces of a Lego set, and so on. The key is to keep the stuff cheap if it's given on a daily basis, but it also has to be viewed as neat and interesting by the child. Dollar stores are great places to find these items, and often a walk through with the child will yield a treasure chest of good ideas.

Older grade-schoolers tend to have more expensive tastes and desire toy or craft supplies that cost too much to be earned on a daily basis. I suggest allowing them to earn daily credit toward a nicer object by using poker chips or tokens to be traded in at a later date for a Lego set, a Barbie doll, an action figure, or a new CD.

Earning money is exciting for all kids—but the amount given differs upon age. Kindergarten and first graders are generally satisfied with a quarter or two, whereas older kids go for the big bucks—a dollar a day that can be saved up for a toy, used to buy ice cream at lunch, or just tucked away for a rainy day is often appreciated.

Clothing is another good material reward to use, although grade-schoolers are not as interested as are preteens and teenagers. However, you can offer a "clothing token" or "clothing poker chip" that can be saved up to trade in later for an item that *you* feel is unnecessary or extravagant, but the *child* feels he can't live without. This may be another baseball cap (although his cap collection is taking over the closet floor) or the latest T-shirt design that your fourth grader just has to have. You're still buying the kid's clothing—these are extras that you're not willing to buy yourself, but will allow your child to foot the bill for having saved the money via tokens.

Middle-schoolers

Young teens seem to live for clothes. Not wearing the latest style of the group she hangs with can often lead your daughter toward social ostracism—a fate not highly regarded by most middle-schoolers. Whether your child is a preppy and craves the latest designer fashions or is a skater and goes for the too-big, too-loose look, the styles that kids choose are very important to them. And that's why daily credit for clothing based upon a good performance at school each day can be so reinforcing. It's also probably cheaper in the long run to have your child earn his own clothes—there will be no impulse purchases on your part and he'll actually learn to budget his money when he realizes that *all* clothing purchases come from the clothing poker chips he earns each day.

Also, you'll save a lot of wear and tear on your stomach lining by never having to say no to his reasonable clothing requests. (The only exception is that you will not allow him to purchase something that he wouldn't be allowed to wear, such as a T-shirt sporting an obscene slogan on it.) All you have to say when you're at the mall and he wants to buy an $80 pair of shorts is: "Sure, just use your clothing poker chips." This system has saved me from many battles with my own two kids—they've learned how to budget (at times the hard way after buying too many shorts and not having enough money left over for a new bathing suit). This system works best when the child has to buy all of his clothing except underwear, socks, winter coats, and specialty items (such as a suit for his cousin's wedding). I also encourage setting an amount for sneakers—those puppies often go for $100 and up, and you may want to set the rule that you'll pay the first $50 and your son can chip in the rest if he wants the more expensive ones. Earning clothing for being responsible for schoolwork is a great idea—it teaches kids budgeting, stops them from whining and hassling you for purchases, and also helps kids to develop a solid work ethic, understanding that hard work earns the things that one wants.

In terms of allowance, middle-schoolers desire money to use for pizza on weekends with their friends, to purchase concert tickets, CDs, movie tickets, and a host of other "necessities." The more money, the better, as far as they're concerned!

High Schoolers

Just like their younger counterparts, teens crave clothing money as well as allowance for other purchases. Add to their list of needs money for gas, cash for dates, and big bucks for food after school. Material reinforcers are very enticing to teens, but again, only if they have to earn it— money will not be important if you're forking over fives and tens just because they are bugging you. If your child knows that all allowance and clothing monies are connected to responsible school behavior, that will get his attention as well as a good school performance.

Negative Consequences

Just as positive consequences need to be important and attractive to the child in order to be effective, so do negative consequences. They must be perceived by the child as *significantly unpleasant* in order to grab the kid's attention to motivate cessation of inappropriate behavior or creation of appropriate action. There are three basic types of negative consequences that work best with kids—the appropriateness of each being dependent on the personality as well as the age of the individual child. The three types are loss of privileges, time-out, and loss of possessions. Let's take a look at privileges first.

Loss of Privileges

The types of privileges that are important to kids vary upon the individual child as well as the age and stage of development.

Grade-schoolers

Young children love to be busy and hate to be bored. They usually push for a later bedtime (either through negotiation or stalling tactics), enjoy playing outside or having a friend over, and using electricity (remember—anything that plugs into the wall or uses batteries). This is the opposite of the positive consequence of activity rewards, so it may be helpful to review that section and consider *taking away* the activity reinforcers that you've decided are important to your grade school age kids.

Middle-schoolers

Taking away freedoms ("restricting" or "grounding") will probably get the attention of your middle-schooler and will promote thinking twice before skipping her homework tomorrow. Preteens and young teens like being able to socialize and grounding to the home really cramps their style. Throw in loss of electricity for a middle-schooler (no telephone, television, or video games) and you'll probably have a motivated kid—especially if you stick to your guns and not cave in to her bugging you to cut the restriction short.

High Schoolers

Even tougher for teens than for younger kids is being stuck at home with the folks, especially without communication with the outside world via visiting friends or talking on the telephone. The trick, though, is to stick with the loss of privilege rule if you've given it to your homework-evading or school-skipping son. If you don't, he'll learn how to play you like a fiddle—looking depressed when restricted, threatening to be more rebellious, or by flat-out telling you that restrictions or loss of electricity won't work. They will work—but only if you do not cave in to any manipulatory maneuvers! Also, loss of driving privileges or the right to spend the night out at a friend's house really hurts! Limits to freedom and socialization tend to be very effective negative consequences, especially to teenagers.

Time-out

The negative equivalent of the positive consequence of affirmation is time-out. Affirmations work by giving the child positive attention, whereas time-out is effective by taking away attention. The effectiveness of time-out varies greatly depending upon the age of the child, and as do all consequences, works best if it is perceived as significant to the individual youngster. The purpose of time-out is to bore the kid, not to harm him—some children enjoy being sent to their room without TV, they can read a novel or play with their toys. Others can't stand isolation and therefore a shorter amount of time-out works well. Many kids whom I speak with report that they prefer Mom or Dad yelling at them or even giving a quick spank rather than to have to endure an *effective* time-out! The key word is *effective*—time-out needs to get the child's attention—because it is lengthy, in an uncomfortable or boring spot, as well as conflicting with engaging in positive activities, such as parent time, watching television, or playing with friends.

Many folks I've spoken with have used time-out in

some fashion, but most often it is used in an ineffective manner. The keys to appropriate time-out are:

- Setting

- Length

- Getting kids into time-out and staying there

- Safety

Lets take a look at the time-out setting first.

Setting

When polled, putting a child in a hall corner or the bedroom tend to be the most popular time-out locations. The problem with the first is that few children will actually stay in a corner, nose to the wall. Most scoot around, flop off of the time-out chair, wiggle into the next room searching for attention or a quick glimpse at the TV set. To die-hard hall corner fans I suggest putting a masking tape square on the floor or carpet. This delineates the time-out boundaries so that the child knows the limits set. That's not a guarantee that he'll stay put, but the taped boundaries may be a helpful reminder.

The bedroom is also a hot spot for time-out. This works well with some kids, they don't like being separated from the rest of the family and can't wait to rejoin the activity. Many children, though, find lots to do in their rooms, even if you restrict television or telephone calling,

there are games, toys, books, and magazines there to enter-
tain them. Some parents who use bedroom time-out restrict the child to sitting on the bed, but many kids will hop
off, grab a book, and sneak it into bed with them. Other
folks try to keep the bedroom as sparse as possible—a lost
cause for most families whose closets are bursting at the
seams and need to keep the kids' stuff in their bedrooms. I
recommend using an alternate safe, boring spot other than
the corner or the bedroom. Many parents of kids grade
school age and older will place them in a guest room, the
porch (assuming good weather), or even a bathroom. If
these spots are employed, be sure that they are *safe*. Remove
all medicines, scissors, cleaning products, and so on, as well
as potential playthings. Mom's sewing kit can act as a craft
activity or the tub toys can become captivating again, even
to a twelve-year-old. Remember, the purpose of time-out
is to bore the child, not to harm him!

Length

In my experience most folks do not insist upon a time-out
period that is long enough to be meaningful to the child
and to be *significantly unpleasant*. A common discipline mis-
conception is that the length of time-out should be equal
to one minute of each year of age. Using this method, the
six-year-old gets six minutes of time-out, the fourteen-
year-old gets fourteen minutes. Often I've found that these
time limits should be doubled. A ten-year-old can easily
endure ten minutes of bedroom time-out—he can't even
finish playing a good game of action figures in that time!

However, twenty to thirty minutes in the bedroom, or better yet a guest room or safe bathroom, will really do the trick and Junior will think twice about leaving his math book at school the next day! Also, consider using a countdown timer placed outside the time-out room so that the child knows that when the buzzer sounds you'll let him leave time-out. This avoids the constant question of "Is it time to come out yet?" echoing from the room. He'll know it's time when the buzzer, placed outside the room, goes off.

Getting Kids into
and Keeping Them in Time-out

It's not always easy to get a kid into time-out and to keep her there. Some kids will voluntarily go into the time-out room when told and wait there patiently until they're allowed to leave. The more ornery variety may refuse to go, and often folks resort to yelling at them or to actually dragging the child into the time-out setting. When working with stubborn critters, I prefer to set a timer and they must beat the buzzer into the time-out room. If they do, that's great and time-out begins. If they do not beat the buzzer, I tell the parents to consider dropping the time-out consequence, but taking and giving away one of the child's important possessions at the next convenient and safe time. The possession discarded must be of interest to the child— giving away one of your daughter's 300+ crayons probably won't bother her, but taking away a Beanie Baby and donating it to a thrift shop or to the Salvation Army probably will get her attention! The possession taken shouldn't be the favorite doll or blanket needed to sleep with, but it should be of importance to the child or she'll continue to give you a hard time getting into time-out. Also, consider using loss of possession for staying in time-out. Instead of holding the door shut as your kid tugs on the other side, just set the rule that if she leaves the time-out spot prematurely, she can come out but faces a permanent loss of possession. This will most likely make her think twice before trying to sneak out of the time-out situation again!

Safety

If you're going to use time-out as a negative consequence, remember to make sure that the setting is safe. Grade-schoolers can inadvertently hurt themselves if scissors or sharp objects are available, or if furniture is unsteady for the timed-out Tarzan. If you're unsure of the safety of the time-out spot, error in terms of being overcautious—either remove or secure the potentially dangerous object or use a different time-out setting. Also, some middle- and high schoolers have been known to escape through bedroom windows in order to avoid time-out, so you may wish to secure these also.

Grade-schoolers Versus Middle- and High Schoolers

Time-out tends to work better for younger kids than for preteens and teens mainly because it's difficult to get a teenager to go and to stay in time-out, whereas younger kids tend to be more compliant. Use of the "beat the buzzer/loss of possession" rule noted above is helpful, though, in getting the older ones into the time-out situation and in keeping them there. In addition, middle- and high schoolers often enjoy being left alone, not having to communicate with their parents or siblings, and they may enjoy a bit of solitude in their bedroom. If this is the case in your home, then a negative consequence other than time-out may prove to be more effective.

Loss of Possession

Just as earning material rewards are terrific positive reinforcers for appropriate academic behavior, loss of possessions can be very effective as negative consequences. Taking and giving away an object (not just putting it up in the closet for a while) really gets the child's attention. I've spoken with many kids who don't really mind the Nintendo being put away, mainly because they know they'll soon be able to use it again, especially if they do a good job of bugging Mom or Dad about it. But *giving* a Nintendo cartridge to the Salvation Army or to a thrift store is a horse of a different color. That really hurts, as game cartridges are expensive and hard to come by.

It's not unusual for parents to initially object to the loss of possession technique, just the idea of "giving away" an expensive item (a necklace or the kid's favorite CD) goes against the grain of frugality. I try to reconcile this conflict by reminding clients of my therapy fees and how losing a few CDs is actually much cheaper than having to see me for three or four more sessions! Parents also feel guilty for taking away something that belongs to the child. To put the guilt into better perspective, I've asked them to consider how awful they're going to feel if their child does not graduate from high school or if his grade-point average is too low to get into his college of choice. Losing a few CDs, necklaces, or Nintendo cartridges is peanuts when compared to living with school failure, dropping out, or having to stay home to attend the local community college rather than going off to school with one's best friend.

The positive and negative consequences discussed above and graphically shown in Figure 3 (page 102) form the bases of motivators available for use when trying to get your child to be responsible regarding schoolwork. These are *external motivators,* and if used correctly will lead to *internal academic motivation* as the youngster inculcates good study habits which eventually become second nature. Remember, consequences, both positive and negative, should be tailored to the individual child. Some will be motivated by positive rewards, others work best by avoiding negative consequences, and still other kids respond best to a combination of both rewards and punishments. Use the combination that works for your child, as well as what is most realistic and convenient for your family.

Kid Human Nature

Like it or not, there are a few laws of human nature that just don't seem to go away. No matter how you package them, use creative semantics, or deny their existence—certain behavioral connections continue to occur. Here's a review of some of the most important laws of kid human nature that pertain to academic achievement.

1. Behaviors that are rewarded tend to continue.

2. Behaviors that are punished generally decrease or cease.

3. Neither of the above holds true unless the rewards or punishments are important to the individual receiving the consequences.

4. Hollow threats are generally seen as meaningless; only those that actually occur produce a change in kid behavior.

5. Even if threats are carried out, this must be done in a consistent manner or the child may gamble and hope that the parent will become distracted and change their mind.

6. Some kids will perform best when both carrots are dangling and the possibility of negative consequences hover over their heads.

7. Consequences must be clear, concise, comprehensive and important in order to work.

8. Grandma's rule (work before play) is always a good fall-back position when the child hits you up with a request and you can't think straight at the moment.

9. You have the right as a parent to say "No."

10. The kid has the right to ask, "Why not?"—but one time only.

11. On occasion "Because I said so" may just have to suffice.

12. If your son or daughter occasionally does not like you, or even hates you at the moment—that's okay. In fact, you're probably doing something wrong if that never occurs.

13. It's better to feel a little guilty now by disappointing your kid and not letting him skip school for the beach volley ball tournament than to feel helpless, humiliated, and downright awful when you're standing with your son before a juvenile judge in truancy court.

14. Your child will try to talk you out of all of the above if given the chance—that's okay, it's kid human nature.

15. Most parents travel this bumpy road—trying to maintain the precarious balance between promoting child independence and self-sufficiency while keeping an eye open for academic slacking off, use of poor judgment, or behavior problems within the classroom.

16. Above all, don't do a parental meltdown—a nonchalant parental attitude, even when you're pushed

to the limit, is much more effective in getting your kid's attention than performing a screaming fit. It catches kids off guard and makes them wonder if you are planning something that they really need to pay attention to!

six

The Study Skills
Program

~~~~~~

L auro Cavasos, Secretary of
Education for President
Ronald Reagan, once noted that "The single best predictor
of academic success is parental involvement." Surprised?
When looking at the research, it was clear to Mr. Cavasos
that the amount of involvement that parents give to a
child's academic career is, on a day-to-day basis, more
important than the child's race, religion, or even socioeco-
nomic status. This finding is of great importance as it suggests that no matter who you are your kids can succeed
academically if you're supervising and guiding them correctly along the way.

The problem is that many kids do not particularly care
if their grades are up to snuff—you may seem to be the
one who's worried about silly things such as grade-point

averages, credits toward graduation, or impressing the teacher with creative or profound answers. Kids, as noted earlier, often have different priorities than do their folks as well as having the incredible ability to rationalize away reality or to use denial, and frankly, to act just plain dumb at times. Why? Well, first try to put yourself in their shoes. What tends to make a kid popular at school? Is it good behavior and superior grades? Probably not for many kids, in fact it tends to be the superficial stuff that is valued more— one's appearance, cool clothes, and a good sense of humor go a long way toward popularity.

So, quit trying to convince yourself that your child *should* care as much as you do about his academic success. He probably doesn't at age ten, thirteen, or even sixteen, but will one day as he begins to recognize the value of education and the doors that it opens. And consider that almost any habit or skill is more easily learned or established the earlier it is begun. Therefore, kindergarteners are at the perfect age to begin to learn appropriate study skills and habits. Although kids in high school benefit greatly, they do so with a bit more grumping and complaining!

Also, keep in mind that most children have developed few, if any, study skills. Somehow they've gotten through grade school with little homework completed, passed middle school by paying attention at times in class, and may be barely slipping by in high school via help from their friends or frantic efforts before finals in order to salvage semester grades.

I've found that the key to getting and keeping good grades is to set up an organizational study program for your child that is realistic, comprehensive, clear, and accountable. If it's too complicated, your daughter may forget to complete it. If it's not clear and comprehensive, some important information may slip through the cracks. And most important, if the organizational system does not allow for easy accountability (a way to check on the accuracy of homework assignments and test schedules), it will be less than successful.

Your daughter may not particularly care about getting organized but would certainly be interested in earning more privileges as well as toning down your nagging about her grades. The end result of an effective study program is that the child's grades improve, parents nag less, the parent-child relationship thrives and when the light finally goes on in the kid's head, her grades are good enough to get into college.

My study skills program has five essential steps:

- Developing and setting up the Daily Assignment Sheet (*DAS*) system for your child.

- Setting up a parent/teacher/child conference to clearly communicate what is expected daily from everyone. (If a conference cannot be accomplished due to teacher workload or the parents' work schedule, then an instruction sheet can be distributed to each teacher explaining the ins and outs of the system. Figure 4 on page 132 is a sample teacher instruction sheet provided for your use.)

- Establishing criteria for earning a *Good Day* on the program.

- Setting up the consequences for earning a *Good Day*.

• Consider using a study partner as an enhancement to the program.

~~~~~~~ Figure 4

Teacher Instructions for the Daily Assignment Sheet (DAS)

The Daily Assignment Sheet (*DAS*) involves my child using a new sheet of paper each day which will list all of his subjects. There is a space on the *DAS* for him to write down (as specifically as possible) the homework assignment for the day, as well as any unfinished classwork that needs to be completed that night. This is to be noted in Column B of the *DAS*. Also, my child places the date that the homework is due in the box following the word "Due." If there is no homework assignment or classwork to be completed that day, my child checks off the "None" box. Column C notes any projects, book reports, tests, and quizzes announced that day and he should write in the appropriate box the topic of the assignment as well as the date due. If there are no new assignments that day, he'll check off the "None" box. At the end of each subject or class, my son will be coming to you, the teacher, to review what he's filled in for Columns B and C. I'm requesting that you sign your name under the appropriate subject in Column A if what my child wrote is accurate. Please do not sign this form if his comments are inaccurate or incomplete. It is not your responsibility to complete it for him, but to tell him what is missing and then he'll complete it and obtain your signature.

Using the *DAS* will benefit everyone, in that my child will become more responsible by noting the work that he must do, and I, the parent, will be able to stay on top of your expectations and make sure that my child completes the work and studies for quizzes and tests.

On Friday, please complete Column D, which asks you to note the number of homework assignments not turned in that week, as well as any test or quiz grades that my child has received. In this way I can double-check that all homework that was completed gets turned in to you. There will be a set of rewards given to my youngster each day if he's earned a *Good Day* and these rewards will be removed if he does not. The rewards, I believe, are significant to my child and will motivate him to work to his potential in your class.

I greatly appreciate your cooperation in this matter. This is a terrific communication tool between school and home and I guarantee that I'll hold up my end of the bargain and give my child positive consequences for appropriate behavior and performance, as well as negative consequences if he does not meet the criteria for a *Good Day*. If you have any questions, please contact me at my home telephone number.

Thank you very much!

Mark's Story

Mark's Folks

Before we began the Daily Assignment Sheet program, we were having difficulties with our thirteen-year-old son. We were talking, but no one was listening. Even yelling didn't accomplish very much in terms of schoolwork and homework. We learned that by having consequences for using a Daily Assignment Sheet, our son found that by listening and taking responsibility for his actions, he would gain privileges (mall trips, movies, and so on.), allowance money, and a self-esteem boost as well. Mark has to be home on time from school, get papers and books ready for beginning his school assignments, and prepare his bookbag for school the next day when he's completed his homework. His grades have improved tremendously! There has definitely been an improvement in our son's behavior and he's more aware of what is expected of him. Responsibility is his key word now.

Mark

Being on the Daily Assignment Sheet program has helped me to behave better at school. I've gotten more organized and studied better. My grades have been A's, B's, and some C's. This is much better than last year. I've learned that I can get my allowance, trip privileges, and clothing allowance if I behave, mind my parents, and learn more responsibility. It's really not as hard to do as I thought at the beginning.

The Daily Assignment Sheet (DAS)

Let's start with setting up the Daily Assignment Sheet (*DAS*) system. A sample *DAS* can be found on page 136, which you can use as the basis for your child's assignment sheet. Also, an example of a completed *DAS* is found on page 137 for your perusal. Since this is a daily form, a new one is to be used each day. The *DAS* contains several columns to be filled in, as well as places for the child to note her name and the date. Column A is titled "Subject/Teacher's Signature." Whether your child is in grade school and has only one or two teachers a day, or is a middle- or high schooler, most kids study five or six subjects a day. On your *DAS* fill in the subject names in Column A as they chronologically occur throughout the day, and make several copies of this form for future use. For example, a grade-schooler's teacher may start the day by presenting reading, spelling, then writing, followed by math, science, and social studies. Each of the subjects is written in order in Column A. Middle- and high schoolers should list their subjects in the order that their classes occur each day. The name of the subject is written in Column A *above* the dashed line, and the space *under* the line is reserved for the teacher's signature (see the sample *DAS* on page 137).

Each day the child writes in all homework assigned for each subject in Column B, which is titled "Homework/Incomplete Classwork." This means that not only are all homework assignments to be noted, but all incomplete classwork that is to be finished at home that night is to be written in also. Each box in Column B also provides a place

~~~ Figure 5
Daily Assignment Sheet (DAS)

Date: _____   Name: _____

A SUBJECT/TEACHER'S SIGNATURE	B HOMEWORK/INCOMPLETE CLASSWORK		C BOOK REPORTS/TESTS/QUIZZES PROJECTS ANNOUNCED	D FRIDAY REPORT
	"None"( )	"Due"( )	Date: Topic: "None"( )	# of H.W. Assignments Missed Quiz & Test Grades
	"None"( )	"Due"( )	Date: Topic: "None"( )	# of H.W. Assignments Missed Quiz & Test Grades
	"None"( )	"Due"( )	Date: Topic: "None"( )	# of H.W. Assignments Missed Quiz & Test Grades
	"None"( )	"Due"( )	Date: Topic: "None"( )	# of H.W. Assignments Missed Quiz & Test Grades
	"None"( )	"Due"( )	Date: Topic: "None"( )	# of H.W. Assignments Missed Quiz & Test Grades
	"None"( )	"Due"( )	Date: Topic: "None"( )	# of H.W. Assignments Missed Quiz & Test Grades

~~~ Figure 6
Example Daily Assignment Sheet (DAS)   Date: _Sept. 22_   Name: _Jonathan_

A SUBJECT/TEACHER'S SIGNATURE	B HOMEWORK/INCOMPLETE CLASSWORK	C BOOK REPORTS/TESTS/QUIZZES/ PROJECTS ANNOUNCED	D FRIDAY REPORT
Algebra *DAJ.*	page 23, odd problems "None" ( ) "Due" (W)	Date: *Sept. 23* Topic: *test, chapter 1* "None" ( )	# of H.W. Assignments Missed *none* Quiz & Test Grades *98% — test*
Earth Science *Mr. Bsham*	"None" (X) "Due" ( )	Date: *Sept. 24* Topic: *Quiz-ch.1, Sections 2+3* "None" ( )	# of H.W. Assignments Missed *none* Quiz & Test Grades *none*
Spanish I *RAP*	"None" (x) "Due" ( )	Date: Topic: "None" (X)	# of H.W. Assignments Missed *section 1 review sheet* Quiz & Test Grades *missed quiz—9/21*
English *Lowell Howard*	Activity sheet on Romeo + Juliet "None" ( ) "Due" (T)	Date: *Oct. 1* Topic: *Book Report— Romeo + Juliet* "None" ( )	# of H.W. Assignments Missed *none* Quiz & Test Grades *92% — quiz*
Art *MSH*	"None" (X) "Due" ( )	Date: *Oct. 2* Topic: *Portfolio to be checked* "None" ( )	# of H.W. Assignments Missed *none* Quiz & Test Grades *none*
U.S. Government *J.G. John*	Read chapter 3 "None" ( ) "Due" (F)	Date: *Sept. 24* Topic: *ch. 3 test* "None" ( )	# of H.W. Assignments Missed *worksheet-ch.3* Quiz & Test Grades *78% — quiz 87% — test*

for the child to check off if there is no homework or incomplete classwork assigned (placing the check in the "None" box) as well as a place to note the due date ("Due"). The latter informs the parent as well as reminds the child when each assignment is to be turned in.

Before moving on to the next subject the child fills in Column C which is labeled "Book Reports/Tests/Quizzes/ Projects Announced." There is room in each box per subject for the child to fill in the topic of the book report, quiz, or test, as well as the day that the project is due or that the test will occur. As in Column B, if no book reports, projects, tests, or quizzes are announced in that subject that day, the child is to check the "None" box in Column C.

Now that Columns B and C are completed, your kid needs to validate that what she wrote down is accurate. To do so, she brings the completed *DAS* to each teacher before leaving each class (or in grade school, before the next subject is begun) and asks the teacher to sign off on the sheet in the appropriate place in Column A. The teacher's signature validates that what the child wrote for homework, projects, tests, and quizzes is accurate and is a great way for the teacher to communicate to you on a *daily basis* what is expected of your child. Remember, the kid fills out Columns B and C, not the teacher! Children should be responsible for noting their expectancies—it is not the teacher's responsibility nor does the teacher have the time to do it.

I suggest to children that they stow the *DAS* in the right-hand pocket of a homework organizer folder as soon as it is signed by the teacher. This folder contains pockets on both the left- and right-hand sides as well as having brads in the middle for the placement of papers. In this way, the odds of losing or misplacing the *DAS* is greatly reduced and the assignment sheet can easily be found to use for the remaining subjects.

Your child continues to fill in the *DAS* in this manner throughout the school day, and middle- and high schoolers should have five, six, or seven teacher signatures (depending upon the school curriculum) by the end of the day. Grade-schoolers may have only one or two teacher signatures each day. Tell your child to check the *DAS* at her locker before leaving school (for grade-schoolers, during the "pack up" time at the end of the day) to make sure that all necessary materials are brought home. Have her run her finger down Columns B and C, which will remind her to bring home, for example, the math book in order to complete problems or the science text in order to be able to answer the questions on the worksheet.

Using this procedure takes the guesswork out of homework—the teachers' signatures validate what has to be done and when it is due. Just think of all of those times that you've asked your child about homework and have received answers, such as "I can't remember" or "I know I have math homework, but I left the book in my locker" (and it's too late to go back to get it). Or how about the old standby of: "I did it in school and turned it in." Sometimes these answers are not only frustrating but downright hard to believe. That's why the *DAS* is so valuable—it puts an end to guesswork as well as serving as a reminder to your child at the end of the day which books and materials need to be brought home.

Okay, so now your daughter is home, has the completed

and signed *DAS* and all of the appropriate books and materials. It's time for her to do her work! Some families allow the child to schedule homework completion as they like— either first going out to play, then completing it after dinner, whereas others prefer the kid to grab a quick snack, take a fifteen- or thirty-minute "let-down" break, and then get started on their studies. There are no fast and firm rules— whatever works for your family is the way to go.

Personally, I prefer children to get it over with so that they can relax later—going out to play, attending sports practice, or chatting on the telephone. This also teaches kids to tackle what they don't particularly want to do *first* and they'll see the payoff via feelings of accomplishment as well as stress reduction—a far cry from the pressure that procrastination often induces.

Now, how do your motivate your child to complete the homework? This is where the principles of behavior management, specifically the positive and negative consequences discussed in Chapter Five, come in. Some previously disorganized kids will fill in the *DAS* and do their homework without need for consequences—these children just needed to be taught an organizational system that's easy to follow. Other students, such as the *if-then*, *rebellious*, and especially those of the *manipulative* variety, respond very well to not only the organizational aspects of the *DAS*, but need daily consequences in order to be motivated to complete the work. I recommend that you tie as many of the positive rewards recommended in Chapter Five to your child having a *Good Day* (the criteria for which will be defined after completely reviewing the *DAS* plan). This means that the appropriateness of the child's school performance as well as homework completion determines the consequences she'll receive each day. But more on that later, I first want to complete the discussion related to getting the homework done, studying for tests, and getting the bookbag ready for the next school day.

Remember that the child is using a "homework organizer" folder, and that today's *DAS* (as well as some blank ones) are to be placed in the right-hand pocket? Good, because there's a place for everything in my study skills program! Teach your child to put *all* other papers that are handed back to her each day in the left-hand pocket. This will contain worksheets, tests and quizzes graded and returned, parent permission forms to be signed and returned, as well as classwork begun but not finished, which is to be completed later at home that day.

When the child starts to do homework, she should begin by removing the *DAS* and surveying what has to be accomplished that afternoon. Perhaps she'll tackle math first, then move on to the science worksheet next. By reviewing Column B, she'll know what's due to be handed in the next day or two, and perusal of Column C informs her of the next scheduled test or quiz, or if any long-term assignments, such as projects or book reports, have been announced.

I suggest completing the work due tomorrow first, then tackling the studying and projects next. This gives the child a feeling of accomplishment and helps put the amount of work left to do into better perspective. Have your child use a red pen and check off each box in Column B as it is completed (even if there was no work assigned and the "None" box was checked). The red checkmark means that the subject has been "dealt with," either by completing the work or by noting that there was none to do. Next, move to Column C regarding book reports, projects, tests, and quizzes announced. If the work or test is occurring tomorrow, have your child get started on it immediately. You'll probably have to quiz grade- and middle-schoolers to make sure that they've done a good job of studying. Some high schoolers may ask for your help, and a short quiz often clarifies what information they know cold and what they need to continue to review. If, in Column C, something is not due for a few days or weeks, have your child write the assignment on a monthly calendar, which is kept either in a visible spot in the child's bedroom or perhaps behind the *DAS* in the right-hand pocket of the homework organizer folder. Some kids prefer the notebook-size variety of monthly calendar that is 8½ x 11 inches and fits easily into the homework organizer pocket. That way they can check long-term assignments or tests while at school. A sample monthly calendar is presented in Figure 7 on page 143.

Instead of just noting on the calendar the day that a book report is due or a test is to occur, I find that it's best to teach your child to break down large projects into smaller units and to note these *daily* on the calendar. For example, a report on a 200-page book that is due in two weeks can be noted on the monthly calendar as follows—write "20 Pages of Napoleon Book" each day for the first ten days (that will complete the reading of the book), note "Begin Rough Draft of Napoleon Book Report" on the eleventh day, followed by "Complete Rough Draft of Napoleon Book Report" on the twelfth day and "Final Draft of

~~~ Figure 7
Monthly Calendar

Month <u>November</u>

SUNDAY	MONDAY	TUESDAY	WEDNESDAY	THURSDAY	FRIDAY	SATURDAY
Date:	Date:	Date:	Date: 11/1	Date: 11/2	Date: 11/3	Date: 11/4
Date: 11/5	Date: 11/6	Date: 11/7 20 Pages of Napoleon Book	Date: 11/8 20 Pages of Napoleon Book	Date: 11/9 20 Pages of Napoleon Book	Date: 11/10 20 Pages of Napoleon Book	Date: 11/11 20 Pages of Napoleon Book
Date: 11/12 20 Pages of Napoleon Book	Date: 11/13 20 Pages of Napoleon Book	Date: 11/14 20 Pages of Napoleon Book	Date: 11/15 20 Pages of Napoleon Book	Date: 11/16 20 Pages of Napoleon Book	Date: 11/17 Begin Rough Draft of Napoleon Book Report	Date: 11/18 Complete Rough Draft of Napoleon Book Report
Date: 11/19 Final Draft of Napoleon Book Report	Date: 11/20 Hand in Napoleon Book Report	Date: 11/21	Date: 11/22	Date: 11/23	Date: 11/24	Date: 11/25
Date: 11/26	Date: 11/27	Date: 11/28	Date: 11/29	Date: 11/30	Date:	Date:

Napoleon Book Report" on day thirteen. Using this system, your child will learn the invaluable study skill of breaking down large projects into smaller, more accessible parts. This combats procrastination and the inevitable cramming at the last minute. This generally leads to greater learning, as psychological studies have shown that distributed practice (reviewing small chunks of material) is much more effective than is massed practice (cramming the night before). Also your child's stress level (as well as your own!) will be reasonable and you won't have to nag nightly, which *both* parent and child dislike immensely.

To complete Column C responsibilities, be sure that your child places a red checkmark in each box as the Column C areas are reviewed. This means that a red check occurs when the material for tomorrow's test is studied adequately and the monthly calendar has been completed in terms of breaking down long-term projects and noting them as daily assignments. This should be done as well for tests that will occur in a week and should be written down each day on the calendar to promote daily review. Also, the child needs to check the box on the daily calendar for today's assignment to make sure that all work on the calendar is completed each day. Even if today's calendar box is empty (meaning that there is nothing extra to study), instruct your child to place a red checkmark there. That assures you when you're reviewing the *DAS* and monthly calendar that your kid "dealt with" not only daily but calendar responsibilities as well.

What if your child, for some reason, can't complete an assignment on the *DAS* or the monthly calendar that day? Ask her to circle that piece of work with a red pen and the two of you can discuss it later in the day. This may occur because she needed additional material from the library, didn't understand the concepts involved, or just ran out of time! Help her to see possible solutions—calling a math-wiz friend for help on the worksheet if the problems are beyond your realm of knowledge or scheduling a trip to the library on the monthly calendar to find the extra resource material. Or the circled item may necessitate a trip to the store for poster board and markers or to a pond to collect water lilies for science class. The point is that it's important for your child to circle an item that she's stumped on—this communicates to you that she needs help in this area in some fashion and you can show her how to accomplish the goal, not just resorting to old habits of giving up or blowing off the assignment because the poster board is not readily available!

Okay, your child has now completed all work on the *DAS* as well as today's box on the monthly calendar and has planned out and written in Column C long-term projects or studying for tests on the monthly calendar. She thinks that she's had a *Good Day*, but not quite! Have her get out her homework organizer folder and check to be sure that there is a blank *DAS* for use tomorrow, placed in the right-hand pocket. The papers that were placed throughout the school day in the left-hand pocket should have been removed, completed as homework, or signed by you to be returned to school. Teach your child to put *all* work to be returned to school the next day in the middle section of the homework organizer. Secure notebook paper in the three brads in the center so that the work does not fall out. Make sure that *all* work stays in the homework organizer—math placed in the math book may get left in the locker and the science worksheet thrown in the book-bag may get lost. (If a paper does not have holes in it, use a three-hole punch so that it can be placed in the brads in the middle section of the homework organizer.) In this way your child will know exactly where to look for papers when the teacher calls for homework to be turned in. No more scrambling around in the bookbag or leafing through texts to find a folded-up math paper. The homework organizer allows your child to go right to the correct spot, pull out the paper, turn it in, and feel like a Junior Einstein. That's precisely why the homework organizer *must go to each class every day* and not be left in the locker or at home. It contains not only homework to be turned in, but perhaps the monthly calendar to review, and also a new *DAS* that needs to be filled in during each subject and signed by each teacher. The value of the homework organizer cannot be overstated—it is a crucial part of my study skills program.

You have probably noticed Column D on the *DAS*. I've purposely waited until you are familiar with Columns A, B, and C before discussing Column D, the "Friday Report." Getting a weekly report from the teacher is invaluable. As you can see, Column D asks *the teacher* to fill in the number of homework assignments the child has failed to turn in *that week* (Monday through Friday), and the grades on any tests or quizzes turned back to the child *that week*. The reason Column D asks for weekly progress versus a cumulative grade to date in each subject is that it gives you specific information. For instance, let's say your son brought home a completed *DAS* for each day this week, with teachers' signatures for each in Column A, and Columns B and C filled out appropriately. You note that there was math homework assigned only on Monday and Thursday and he checked the "None" box for math on Tuesday and Wednesday. Also, Monday's Column C for social studies noted that a test would occur on Thursday, covering chapters seven and eight in the text. You remember that he studied Tuesday and Wednesday nights for social studies and you quizzed him each day to ascertain whether he needed further review. There were no other quizzes or tests announced on the *DAS* for the week.

However, on today's *DAS* (Friday) the math teacher reports in Column D that the homework assigned on Tuesday and Wednesday was not turned in, that your son earned a B on the social studies test yesterday, and to your surprise, his English teacher noted an F for a test taken earlier that day! How could this have happened? Column A was signed by the math teacher on Tuesday and Wednesday, when your son noted no homework in Column B. How could he have not turned in homework if none was assigned? There are only three possible answers—your son is a budding counterfeiter and forged the teacher's signature or, more likely, the teacher signed off on the *DAS* in Column A without really looking at it closely, not noticing that your child checked the "None" box for homework when there really was some assigned or your child did the homework and forgot to turn it in. All are possible and I've seen these behaviors frequently. The *manipulative student* can be great at forging signatures and the *disorganized student* may not always notice the assignment on the board, check the "None" box, and not realize that the teacher signed off incorrectly in Column A on the *DAS*. The *disorganized student* also tends to forget to turn in his homework, but if you review with her that it's placed in the center brads of the homework organizer, she'll most likely get in the habit of looking for it there.

How about the B in social studies? That's a good grade and could have been predicted because you knew about the test in advance and helped your son by quizzing him after he reviewed the chapters. But what about the F on the English test? Where did that come from? Most likely, again, from either a forged teacher signature (the kid didn't want to study English Monday night because his favorite shows were on TV) or the teacher signed the *DAS* that day without reviewing what your child wrote in Columns B and C, not noticing that the test information was omitted.

The solution to these problems is simple—have a chat with the teacher to ascertain whether she's signing at times without appropriate review of the *DAS* or whether the kid is forging. If the former is the case, just talking with the teacher often will solve the problem—she'll be more careful to review Columns B and C before putting her name on the paper in Column A. However, if forgery is the culprit, it gets a little trickier. I've found three practical ways of handling this issue. First, tell the kid to knock it off—that if you find him forging signatures again, he'll lose his CD player *permanently* to the Salvation Army. Second, get a list of all teachers' signatures and be careful to check them on a daily basis, making sure that they're accurate. If you're concerned that one looks fishy, call the teacher at home that night or at school the next day to check it out. Just knowing that you're on to him may stop this sneaky behavior in its tracks! Third, if ideas one and two either do not appeal to you or you've tried them and they don't work, consider giving each of the teachers a small, self-inking stamp, which you can purchase inexpensively at a craft or office supply store. For example, the math teacher gets a stamp with a star on it, English gets a smiley face stamp, and the science uses a unicorn. Instead of signing their name, they stamp the *DAS* in Column A. Your son will have trouble duplicating these designs and his forgery days will be history!

Criteria for Earning a Good Day

Now that you understand the workings of the *DAS*, it's time to set the criteria for earning a *Good Day* on the program. If a child earns a *Good Day*, he will receive positive reinforcers; if not, negative consequences are in order (this may be a good time to review these sections in Chapter Five). To have earned a *Good Day* the youngster must have accomplished *all* of the following expectations:

- Completed the *DAS*, which means that none of the boxes are empty (*all* teachers have signed off unless the child wasn't in that class that day for an appropriate reason), and Columns B and C are filled in accurately or the "None" box is checked. On Friday Column D must also be filled in by the teachers, not the kid. (If the child "forgets" to bring home the *DAS*, the *Good Day* is forfeited.)

- All materials (books, folders, worksheets) as noted on the *DAS* as necessary for homework and study completion are to be brought home. (A perfectly completed *DAS* does little good if the Spanish book is left at school and there's work to be done in it!)

- The child completes *all* of the homework and studying noted as necessary in Columns B and C, as well as in today's spot on the monthly calendar. And this is done in a reasonably civil manner (not too much grumping and complaining). The monthly calendar is filled out for the future and the *DAS* and today's monthly calendar have red checks in all boxes, denoting that all work has been completed. Any red circled items (meaning that the kid needs help in some fashion to complete these tasks) are to be discussed and dealt with by the parent.

- The homework organizer is readied and packed in the bookbag along with any other materials needed for school the next day. Remember, the right side of the homework organizer contains the new *DAS* and perhaps the monthly calendar. The left side should now be empty, since all of today's papers have been either filed in subject folders, completed as homework and placed in the brads in the center of the organizer to be turned in, parent permission slips are signed and also put in the brads for easy accessibility, and unnecessary papers have been thrown away.

That's it—only these four steps need to be taken each school day and your child is on the road to not only good grades but to developing the excellent study habits, skills, and organization that will take her successfully from kindergarten through college!

Consequences for Earning a Good Day

Now that we've established that your kid needs to meet all four of the above criteria in order to have a *Good Day* (not one, two, or three but all four must be accomplished for my study skills program to work), let's talk about consequences. If your daughter achieves a *Good Day*, I suggest that she receive *all five* of the following positive consequences:

➢ **A red allowance poker chip** to be used in any legitimate fashion. This means that she can spend her allowance money on anything that she wants to as long as you allow the item in your home (you may restrict CDs, noting "parental supervision required," and therefore she can't buy these, or perhaps you're restricting her sugar intake and will only allow her to buy one candy bar per week). Other than restricted items, it's her money and she should be allowed to spend it as she likes! She'll soon learn to budget, especially if you become tight as a tick with money and refuse to give her extra or to buy her things on a whim. She receives her allowance chip daily by earning a *Good Day*. I suggest using a poker chip rather than actual money only because it's inconvenient to have cash available each school day. She saves up her red allowance chips and trades them in to you for cash when she's ready to make her purchase.

➤ **A blue clothing poker chip** worth a certain amount of money toward clothing purchases is also enticing to many kids. There are three ways to effectively use the blue clothing poker chip. The first is for preteens and teens—I suggest that you cease to buy their clothing (except for underwear, socks, and special event outfits) and let them choose how they wish to spend their clothing poker chip money. You should not veto a purchase unless it is for a garment that you wouldn't allow your child to wear, such as a T-shirt with an obscene logo on it or a much-too-skimpy bikini that your daughter should never, in your opinion, be old enough to wear. The blue clothing chip should be worth a significant amount of money, since this is the only way that your child can earn clothing. The second option, which targets younger children or teens who don't especially value clothing, is to make the blue clothing poker chip worth much less and is used for "extra" or "unnecessary" clothing items. You'll still be purchasing the bulk of her clothing, but your ten-year-old daughter can save up her blue clothing chips and use them to buy a T-shirt that she doesn't really need but desires, an accessory hat, or her third pair of sneakers. The third option is to use the blue chip not for clothing (if your kid couldn't care less about what he wears) and to earmark it for a special purpose such as a remote control car, horseback riding lessons, or a new computer to be saved up for and purchased in the future.

➤ **A white privilege chip** can be earned, which is saved up and traded in at a later date for various activities or privileges. The family sets up a list of activities desired by the child as well as the number of white privilege chips needed to engage in the activity. For instance, the child may have to pay seven chips to go to a movie, three chips to rent a video, five chips to go out to dinner at his favorite fast-food place, thirty chips to go to a concert, or eight chips to have a few friends spend the night. Other suggested activities are going to the park, bowling, minigolfing—just about anything that your child likes to do. I suggest that the number of chips needed for each activity be based upon the amount of money that the event will cost as well as the length of parent time involved. Be creative, try to include in the list whatever the kid wants to do—it doesn't really mean that he's going to earn the 3,000 chips necessary to go to Disney World! It's a neat way to *earn* privileges rather than to just be handed them, and kids seem to enjoy this reward immensely.

➤ **Electricity** is the privilege to use anything that either plugs into the wall or uses batteries. This is a vast list and includes the use of television, computers, video games, watching video tapes, using the telephone, and playing handheld games. Don't forget that using a remote control car also involves batteries and would fit into this category! (I never take away the electrical devices of lights, blow dryers, and alarm clocks.) Kids hate to lose electricity because it's boring and that is why this is a consequence of such importance.

➤ **Play Time/Freedom**—this is the child's privilege of going outside and playing with or hanging around friends, or having them come over. For grade-schoolers this may take the form of playing tag, board games with friends, climbing the tree house, and so forth. For older kids this usually means hanging around in some fashion, whether they're playing video games in the family room or sitting on their friend's stoop talking. For high schoolers freedom includes getting the keys to the car and going places. Play time or freedom is a very important privilege for kids, one that they really don't like losing.

Giving children the five rewards suggested above daily can be very powerful. The *red allowance chip, blue clothing chip, white privilege chip, electricity*, and *play time/freedom* privileges are terrific reinforcers to use and I would suggest giving all five to the child if she earns a *Good Day* in regard to her school work. If she does not, I would take away all five for that day. This means that she would not received the red, blue, or white poker chips and would not have any electricity or play time/freedom for the rest of that day. The child begins the next day with a "clean slate," looking forward to earning a *Good Day* in regard to her school work and therefore earning the five available rewards that day.

Finally, let's take a look at the *study partner* concept that can be used in conjunction with the *DAS*. A study partner is generally a high school honor student whom you either pay per hour for tutoring your child or who works for service hours needed for a program at school. Many kids in honors programs need to accumulate between 75 and 300 service hours before graduation in order to receive certain scholarships. Most schools will give service hour credit for being a study partner to your child. You can check this out by contacting a guidance counselor or the teacher/sponsor of the National Honor Society at your local high school.

Other ways of finding a study partner are to contact youth leaders at your local church or to place an ad on various bulletin boards where teenagers frequent. My guess is that your child will enjoy working with an older teenager rather than with an adult. Kids make a connection with teens and rarely give them a hard time about studying because their pride is at stake. Your child will not want to humiliate himself in front of an older teenager and will most likely form a bond with this person. Incidentally, study partners also make great role models! If you cannot find a teenager as a study partner, you may consider talking to a neighbor who wouldn't mind working with your child. Just as it's often easier to have somebody else teach your child to drive (parents tend to become very uptight when dealing with their own kids), your child may behave better for a tutor other than yourself. I've had clients whose parents have swapped and worked as study partners for each other's child. Kids may be more polite to an adult other than their own parent, and the work will be completed more efficiently.

The study partner is an enhancement to the *DAS* and organizational system discussed above and is not a necessity. So if you have difficulty finding a study partner, working with your child using the *DAS* is perfectly acceptable although usage of the study partner tends to take some pressure off of your relationship with your kid. If you do use a study partner, make sure that this person is knowledgeable about how the *DAS* is employed, including usage of the monthly calendar. The study partner should alert you each day as to whether the child has completed all five of the necessary components for having a *Good Day*, and if

Nathan's Story

Nathan's Folks

I've found Dr. Peters's study partner method to be extremely helpful in enabling our high school age son to develop organizational skills and other good study habits. These study habits include the consistent use of Dr. Peters's daily, weekly, and monthly planning sheets and end of the week report instead of relying on his memory to recall homework assignments and due dates. He has also developed increased patience. He no longer rushes through assignments. He carefully reviews for each test.

Our son's success is due largely to the involvement of a study partner, an older and very successful student whom Dr. Peters trained to assist our son in this process. The study partner spends approximately four afternoons each week at our home guiding Nathan through his homework assignments and test preparation. He emphasizes the need for organization and shows our son the organizational methods he has utilized in his own work. He guides our son in decision-making. He has become our son's role model. Our son enjoys his company. Our son eagerly anticipates his meetings with his study partner.

Our utilization of Dr. Peters's program is enabling our son to improve his grades and is enhancing his self-esteem. Until we began this program, our son was not a successful student. Assignments were frequently turned in late or not at all. Test scores were poor. His self-esteem was low. Ongoing sessions with tutors and specialists were unsuccessful. This program has changed our son's life.

Nathan

Dr. Ruth Peters's method worked great. Dr. Peters taught me how to study and helped me develop a strong work ethic. I worked with a study partner four times a week. The study partner and I worked on homework and studied for tests and quizzes. He did not just assist me in getting better grades, but provided me with advice about academic and social problems also.

your child has succeeded, then he will receive the three poker chips, freedom, and electricity from you. If it's not a *Good Day*, you withhold these five rewards from your child.

There are times when the five standard rewards are not as effective, though, as I'd like them to be. Some kids seems to be able to live without allowance money or clothing money privileges, as well as freedom or electricity. These children are rare and most will be tempted by the reward system and decide to play ball. With especially ornery kids,

Natalie's Story

Natalie's Folks

The effect of our excellent study partner is that I am removed from the homework process. This responsibility is assumed by our daughter, Natalie and the study partner facilitates the completion of the work. When I was working alone on homework with our daughter, it was frustrating for us both. It took a lot of energy out of me and arguing was damaging to our relationship. The Daily Assignment Sheet helped to organize my daughter and to also establish clear communication between the teachers and myself.

Natalie

My self-esteem has improved because I am now working up to my potential. The effect of the study partner has not only helped me with my schoolwork but also with my attitude. Before, when I sat down to speak with Mom, we would start yelling at each other. Now, both of us can actually speak to each other without getting in screaming fits.

though, I suggest that you may have to play *hardball* and perhaps use *loss of possession* in addition to the five standard consequences. This would mean that on any day that the child did not earn a *Good Day*, not only would he lose his three poker chips, electricity, and freedom, but you would take a significantly important possession away and give it permanently to an association such as the Salvation Army or Goodwill. Most kids will cave in when this occurs, and you will have a motivated student who will use the *DAS* and successfully fulfill *Good Day* requirements, if only to avoid loss of privileges, money, clothing, electricity, freedom/playtime, as well as loss of a possession. As I noted in Chapter Five, you need to be consistent. If you let your child get away with receiving rewards when he hasn't earned the *Good Day*, the message that you're sending is that you're inconsistent and you may find that your kid prefers to roll the dice, hoping that you'll not check to see if it's a *Good Day* and give the rewards. Also, remember to check his *DAS* to be sure that everything's completed as well as the monthly calendar *on a daily basis*.

So are you ready to start the study skills program? Be sure to make out a shopping list and purchase red pens, a monthly calendar, a three-hole punch, a homework organizer folder, and a set of poker chips for use in the system. You may also wish to purchase a countdown timer for grade school kids. Often these children need their homework timed in order to get them going. For instance, you may set the timer for thirty minutes in which your daughter must complete the twenty math problems. Or fifteen minutes may be allowed for her to review her *DAS*, decide what work has to be done, and to begin the actual home-work process. Use of a timer is a terrific motivating device and will stop a large portion of parental nagging, as well as motivating your child to begin the homework and study-ing process each day.

Also, let's take a minute to look at the type of study en-vironment that you may wish to set up for your child. Some kids need parental supervision in order to get them started and to stay on task, which is the case for many grade-schoolers and middle-schoolers. By high school most kids wish to do their homework in the bedroom and usually are quite successful at this. Grade-schoolers, though, tend to need Mom or Dad checking on them every so often to make sure that they are continuing their work. Therefore, you may wish to set grade- and middle-schoolers at the kitchen table (if it's a reasonably quiet spot) so that you can easily check in with them to see how they're doing.

Whether the child's study environment is set in a per-fectly quiet location or one where he'll be exposed to music, television, noise, and so forth, is a personal decision. It's probably a good idea not to have blaring music at the same time that the child is completing his work, but many kids are able to get their work done with some music and background noise. Additionally, consider that when your child leaves for college and lives in a dormitory atmosphere it will most likely be quite noisy. If he or she is used to some degree of noise (TV, music, people talking, and so on), they'll have an easier time adapting to dormitory life and will not have to isolate themselves in the library in order to get their work done.

I've found that kids do not need a special desk and tons of office equipment to do a good job with homework. I've had many parents say to me that they've purchased a beautiful desk and have staplers, markers, a pencil sharpener, and all kinds of gadgets ready for their kids, yet the child still does not do his homework. No gadget is going to motivate your child to complete the work! What will motivate are the consequences that he or she will receive if the *Good Day* is earned based upon the *DAS*, the monthly calendar, and the homework organizer as described in my program. Therefore, don't worry about spending a lot of money on furniture and office equipment. I'd rather see you spend more time supervising and guiding your child regarding homework completion!

Using the DAS for Behavioral Problems as Well as Organizational Difficulties in School

In addition to using the *DAS* to gather information on what homework is due, as well as when the next book report, project, test, or quiz is occurring, another usage is for checking on your child's behavior in class. If your youngster is not participating in class or is misbehaving, you can use the alternate *DAS* provided on page 000 in order to track the behavioral difficulties.

On this form you'll see that Column D notes whether the homework was turned in each day, as the teacher fills this out by checking the box as "Y" for yes, "N" for no, or

~~~ Figure 8

Daily Assignment Sheet (DAS-Alternate)

Date: _____   Name: _____

A SUBJECT/TEACHER'S SIGNATURE	B HOMEWORK/ INCOMPLETE CLASSWORK	C BOOK REPORTS/ TESTS/QUIZZES/ PROJECTS ANNOUNCED	D HOMEWORK TURNED IN? YES NO N/A	E CLASS WORK S U	F CLASS BEHAVIOR S U	G FRIDAY REPORT
	"None" ( ) "Due" ( )	Date: Topic: "None" ( )				# of H.W. Assignments Missed Quiz & Test Grades
	"None" ( ) "Due" ( )	Date: Topic: "None" ( )				# of H.W. Assignments Missed Quiz & Test Grades
	"None" ( ) "Due" ( )	Date: Topic: "None" ( )				# of H.W. Assignments Missed Quiz & Test Grades
	"None" ( ) "Due" ( )	Date: Topic: "None" ( )				# of H.W. Assignments Missed Quiz & Test Grades
	"None" ( ) "Due" ( )	Date: Topic: "None" ( )				# of H.W. Assignments Missed Quiz & Test Grades
	"None" ( ) "Due" ( )	Date: Topic: "None" ( )				# of H.W. Assignments Missed Quiz & Test Grades

"N/A" indicating that no homework was due. (As noted earlier, some kids do the homework and forget to turn it in!) Column E asks the teacher whether the child's class participation was appropriate and the teacher marks an "S" for satisfactory or a "U" for unsatisfactory. Column F is also filled out by the teacher and concerns whether the child appeared to be on-task in the class and displaying good behavior. Again, the teacher notes this by "S" or "U." Column G is the "Friday Report" as noted in the standard *DAS* system.

If you're using the alternate *DAS* for behavioral/participation problems, you may wish to add to the *Good Day* requirements that the child can receive only one or two unsatisfactory marks per day from all of his subjects combined, and that Column D (noting homework turned in) has no more that one "N" marked. (An "N/A" is fine, since if there was no homework to turn in, the child should not be penalized.) If you do add this criteria, make sure that it's fair and clear to the child so that earning a *Good Day* is a realistic possibility.

Using the DAS with Kindergarteners and First Graders

I've frequently used the *DAS* with children in second through twelfth grades. Second, third, fourth, and fifth graders, as noted above, do not change classes six times a day and therefore do not have six teachers to sign off on the *DAS*. However, the one, two, or three teachers they do have each day can check it and sign off on the *DAS* as the various subjects are completed throughout the day. However, kindergarten and first graders may have difficulty with the complexity of the standard *DAS* and I suggest using a much simpler version. A new sheet of paper is used each day and taped to the child's desk. This involves a set of smiley faces, followed by one "frowny face" in a box, drawn on a sheet of paper. Each time the child behaves inappropriately the teacher crosses off one of the smiley faces. For example, if eight smiley faces are placed on the sheet, the ninth would be the frowny face placed at the bottom of the sheet in a square. (A sample Smiley Face Chart is shown as Figure 9 on page 165.) The child is told that as long as the frowny face is not crossed out, he will have earned a *Good Day* and will receive his rewards later that day at home. If the frowny is crossed out (after all the smiley faces have been lost), he'll not have a *Good Day* and will lose all of his daily rewards. In addition, the child should write any homework assignments in the box headed "Homework and Incomplete Classwork" and projects, book reports, tests, or quizzes announced in the other box (both are located at the bottom of the Smiley Face chart). The child is to write in the assignments or announced projects, book reports, tests, or quizzes or to check in the "None" box for either area. The teacher signs off each day, which validates that the number of smiley faces crossed out was a good indicator of behavior, as well as that what the child wrote for homework is correct. In this way, you can keep track of your child's homework as well as his behavior each day and reward him commensurate with his academic and behavioral performances. If your kindergartner or first grader is

~~~~ Figure 9
Smiley Face Chart (SFC)

Name:_____   Date:_____

HOMEWORK AND INCOMPLETE CLASSWORK	PROJECTS, BOOK REPORTS, TESTS, QUIZZES ANNOUNCED
	"Due": "None" ( )
	Teacher Comments:
"DUE": "NONE" ( )	

Madeline's Story

Our daughter, Madeline, was having trouble staying on task in the classroom. She would fidget, play with her hair, and not complete her work. It was obvious that she was easily distracted. These actions eventually got her into trouble, as her teacher felt that our daughter was choosing to just not pay attention. We met with Dr. Peters and discussed our daughter's situation. She suggested a type of behavior modification. Every day a quarter sheet of paper was placed on our daughter's desk. On that sheet I drew smiley faces (the number of smiley faces determined by Dr. Peters). At the bottom of the sheet I drew one frowny face. Each time the teacher had to bring our daughter back on task, she would cross out a face. This practice, I felt, was very helpful because my daughter was able to look down at her desk to be reminded that she had to try to pay attention and she could see how successful she was on that day. I was concerned this may cause embarrassment and/or draw negative attention to her in the classroom. It was handled in a very positive way by her teacher and as her parents we rewarded her for not losing the frowny face. This system of behavior management has worked for our daughter . . . we're still using it. It does not bother her or embarrass her. She tells me that when she looks at the paper on her desk, it helps her to remember to pay attention.

not displaying any behavioral problems in the classroom, then you can skip the smiley face portion of the system and just use the homework assignment sections of the page.

I have had extremely good success with this program, as kids seem to "get it together" when they know that Mom and Dad are going to be made aware of their classroom behavior on a daily basis, as well as finding out what homework they actually have. You can also start your child using a homework organizer folder in kindergarten and first grade. Although this is not as necessary as with the older kids, it sets a good example right from the beginning, and as noted above, most good behaviors are easier to form the earlier that they are begun. In addition, you'll probably have greater cooperation starting my study skills program with little kids rather than waiting until the child is in the eleventh grade. If you begin when he's young, it will be seen as a natural event in his life, one that is expected to begin each fall and to last throughout the school year.

How Long Does My Child Use the Study Skills Program?

Many parents ask how long usage of the program is necessary, and the best answer is: "However long the child needs it." Some kids can use the program for a year and it will click, and over time they'll choose which organizational tools they'll continue to use. Other children need to utilize it for their entire school careers in order to continually motivate them to perform, as well as to behave appropriately in school. Still others profit from usage of a study partner continually through high school. Don't worry—neither the study skills program nor the study partner is a crutch—these systems provide techniques and skills to your child that are invaluable to learn and use as a youngster and are often generalized into their adult lives. Many of us use mentors or coaches as adults to help us to learn a new skill or to motivate us to continue to persist in completing our tasks. Why not give this gift to our children, especially as they're developing their individual work ethic?

seven

Helping Kids in
Special Situations

~~~~~

Kids who are either unmo-
tivated, disorganized, or
both usually respond very well to my study skills program
when both the *DAS* and effective consequences are employed. Grades improve, parents nag less, and the general
home atmosphere is a much more pleasant environment.
However, there are some special situations that result in a
child not working to his potential that are not based in lack
of motivation or disorganization. Often these children are
trying hard in school but due to certain circumstances
seem to be moving one step forward and two steps back-
ward.

The three types of kids who tend to fall into this category are children who have gaps in their learning due to a
variety of personal family situations, kids diagnosed as hav-

ing Attention Deficit Disorder, or those who evidence specific learning disabilities. Let's take a look at children who have missed out on some academic basics in their early school years first.

Knowledge Gaps

Kids develop gaps in knowledge fundamentals for a variety of reasons, and because their academic foundation is so shaky, they tend to have difficulty with learning higher level concepts. These children may have missed school due to a severe illness and the home study program was either inadequate or even nonexistent, or perhaps a parent's job necessitated several moves during the early grade school years. Often if the latter case is the culprit, the child may have reviewed all the math facts twice, but missed out on some of the basic phonic rules due to the transitions. Or there may have been marital stress in the household during kindergarten, first, or second grade, and Mom and Dad were too distracted to keep up with the child's schoolwork and gaps in knowledge developed. These children are often bright, inquisitive youngsters who want to succeed, but it's difficult for them to deal with vowel blends correctly when they're not sure of vowel sounds in isolation. Sounding out a word when you don't know the "*long e*" rule is tough and often leads to poor reading comprehension as well as poor self-esteem. It's very stressful when your child stumbles through reading a passage aloud in class, listening to snickers from the back of the room. And learning multiplication is nearly impossible for the child who never quite memorized the times tables, as the teacher in Texas was just beginning multiplication yet, upon moving to Florida, your son found that the class was finishing up the sevens tables and moving on to the eights.

I've found that the best way to remediate gaps in knowledge is to take the child back to the weak areas and to teach these areas as if it's the first time he's been exposed to them. Your school will be able to administer an academic assessment clarifying his strengths and weaknesses, or you can have a private learning center or psychologist administer an academic achievement battery. Once you know specifically where the gaps are occurring, you'll have the basis for a good remediation plan. Either you or a tutor can work with the child to bring him up to snuff in these areas, filling in the gaps in his knowledge. You'll be amazed at how quickly he'll catch on to high-lever concepts once the basics have been fortified.

Attention Deficit Disorder

The second type of child who does not work to his academic potential, yet appears to be motivated, is the youngster diagnosed with Attention Deficit Disorder (ADD). Kids with true ADD often evidence significant distractibility, concentration difficulties, and impulsivity, especially in situations that they perceive as either boring or tedious—namely, school. These kids often can be found daydreaming, doodling, or frantically trying to catch up to the page the teacher is lecturing from (because the air conditioner noise distracted him and he lost his place in the book!). It's frustrating to give it your all in class, yet somehow consistently fall behind and never quite stay on top of the classwork. Also, kids with true ADD tend to be impulsive, which leads to disorganization. Necessary materials are not always brought home in order to do homework and these children often forget what homework has been assigned that day.

Not only is this frustrating to the child, but it's maddening to the parent. Daily reminders of bringing home the necessary books and keeping track of assignments seem to go unheeded and homework time is usually an unpleasant experience. Even if the child gets started properly on the math paper, you can bet it will still be incomplete a half hour later as you find your daughter staring out the window rather than tackling the problems. True ADD is best dealt with through three channels—medication (via a pediatrician, a child neurologist, or a child psychiatrist), behavior management using a form of my study skills program, and academic assessment and remediation to fill in the gaps in knowledge that have occurred due to inattention to teacher presentations.

Depending upon the source of the statistics, the number of school-age children who have been diagnosed as having Attention Deficit Disorder range from 3 to 5 percent (Ch.A.D.D.) to 10 to 12 (United Nations Commission) percent of boys aged six to fourteen years. Although the causes of Attention Deficit Disorder are still not totally clear, most psychologists feel that this disorder is due to a neurobiological condition. Reduced metabolism rate in the area of the brain specializing in attention, motor control, and inhibition of responses was found in a *New England Journal of Medicine* study. This study dealt with the result of a National Institute for Mental Health research program that used PET scans comparing the brain metabolism of adults with ADD versus those without ADD. These results suggest a neurotransmitter substance imbalance in individuals diagnosed with this disorder.

In an effort to "balance" the neurotransmitters, many physicians have used methylphenidate (Ritalin and its generic versions) as well as other psychostimulants, and, more recently, antidepressant medication. The results are generally positive, although there are some side effects that need to be considered. Specifically, most individuals taking Ritalin for ADD face some amount of insomnia if the medication is taken too late in the day, as well as reporting appetite suppression, especially at lunchtime. There appear to be no significant long-term side effects from stimulant medication usage, as reported by Gabrielle Weiss and Lily Trokenberg-Hechtman in *Hyperactive Children Grown Up*. However, these researchers indicate that approximately one third to one half of children with ADD continue to have some difficulties into adulthood. Specifically, these adults tend to have shorter attention spans, lower impulse control, and more mood swings than do individuals without ADD.

According to the fourth edition of the *Diagnostic and Statistical Manual of Disorders*, Attention Deficit Disorder has three subtypes:

1. Hyperactive/Impulsive
2. Inattentive
3. Combined (meeting criteria for both of the above types)

According to the *Diagnostic and Statistical Manual of Disorders*, the symptoms of Attention Deficit Disorder must have begun before age seven and occur in at least two settings such as school, church, or home. The criteria for diagnosing any of the three types of ADD are that the youngster evidences six or more of the following symptoms for at least six months to such a degree that it is inconsistent with the youngster's appropriate developmental level. These symptoms, according to the *Manual*, are:

Hyperactive-Impulsive Type

HYPERACTIVE

1. Often fidgets with hands or feet, or squirms in seat.

2. Often leaves seat in classroom or another situation in which remaining seated is expected.

3. Often runs about or climbs excessively in situations in which it's inappropriate (in adolescents or adults, may be limited to subjective feelings of recklessness).

4. Often has difficulty playing in leisure activities quietly.

5. Is often on the go or often acts as if driven by a motor.

6. Often talks excessively.

IMPULSIVE

1. Often blurts out answers before questions are completed.

2. Often has difficulty awaiting their turn.

3. Often interrupts or intrudes on others (for example, butts into conversations or games).

These kids are fairly easy to diagnose, in that their behavior tends to be disruptive in the classroom. They are fidgety, get out of their seats often, their work tends to be very impulsive and sloppy, and they seem to have more accidents than other children because they're on the go and not particularly planful.

Inattentive Type

1. Often fails to give close attention to details or makes careless mistakes in schoolwork, housework, or other activities.

2. Often has difficulty maintaining attention to tasks or play activities.

3. Often does not seem to listen when spoken to directly.

4. Often does not follow through on instructions and fails to finish school work, chores, or duties (not due

to oppositional behavior or failure to understand instructions).

5. Often has difficulty organizing tasks and activities.

6. Often avoids, dislikes, or is reluctant to engage in
   tasks that require sustained mental effort (such as
   schoolwork or homework.)

7. Often loses things necessary for tasks or activities
   (for example, toys, school assignments, pencils,
   books, or tools).

8. Is often easily distracted by extraneous stimuli.

9. Is often forgetful in daily activity.

It is much more difficult to diagnose the child with the
inattentive type of ADD than with the hyperactive type.
These children tend to be well-behaved, but are often described as "spacey," "out of it," or "in a cloud." Because the
inattentive, nonhyperactive type of child is not disruptive,
diagnosis often does not occur until later in the grade
school years, whereas the hyperactive youngsters are generally identified by first or second grade.

Combined

Children with combined hyperactive-impulsive and
inattentive Attention Deficit Disorder meet the criteria for
both of these types. That is, they not only have behavioral
problems (including impulsivity and distractibility) but

they tend to get off track easily due to inattention and day-dreaming. These kids are usually diagnosed early in their grade school years. As noted above, the three accepted methods of treating kids with Attention Deficit Disorder tend to be medication, behavior management, and academic remediation.

The Willfully Noncompliant Child

Before jumping to the conclusion that your child may have true ADD, it's often best to make the distinction between the youngster who evidences ADD symptoms versus the child who looks and acts like an ADD kid at school, but whose problems are not neurobiochemical, but rather behavioral in nature. Both types of children can act and perform the same in class as well as during homework time, but the acid test in differentiating the two is that the child with true ADD tries to pay attention, yet has difficulty sustaining concentration. The willfully noncompliant or uncaring kid purposefully avoids doing the work or reading along with the class. This willfully noncompliant child understands teacher directions, can do the work, yet purposefully engages in other activities (doodling, writing notes, playing with the buttons on his shirt) in an effort to kill time until the teacher moves on to a subject that's more interesting to him.

At home the willfully noncompliant child may reluctantly begin to do his work, yet try to sneak in a game of Nintendo, Hang-Man, or engage you in conversation just

to avoid completing the science worksheet. Also, this
sneaky critter leaves his books at school as well as the assignment sheet in an effort to avoid having to do the work
at home. That is, he doesn't "forget" the materials, he purposefully leaves them at school but may use forgetting as an
excuse. As you can see, both kids' work product looks the
same—incomplete classwork, books remaining at school,
and dawdling during homework time, but one child (the
one with true ADD) is not planning to goof up, whereas
the willfully noncompliant kid uses disorganization and
off-task behavior as a way to avoid getting down to work.

How does one distinguish which type of kid is living in
your home? Many psychologists will perform a battery of
tests consisting of an IQ evaluation, several cognitive processing tests, as well as an academic achievement assessment. This information can be helpful, but often the child
with true ADD will pass the test battery with flying colors,
as it's usually given in a quiet, nondistracting environment
with one-on-one attention from an adult evaluator. In my
experience, only the most extreme ADD kids will flunk
these tests under these circumstances. So if your child has
mild or moderate ADD, it may not show up on this time-
consuming as well as very expensive battery of tests.

I've found that the best way to determine if the child
truly has ADD and is evidencing actual concentration difficulties, distractibility, and/or impulsivity (even though he's
trying to control these behaviors and is motivated to work
hard) is to use a behavior management technique that I've
developed and employed for well over twenty years. It's
simple, convenient, and distinguishes the willfully noncompliant critters from the real McCoy. This involves using

a technique similar to my study skills program, but one that concentrates specifically on ADD-like behaviors. *The Daily Report Card (DRC)* is presented as Figure 10 on page 180. As you can see from perusal of the *DRC*, there are ten behaviors that are targeted as problem areas. The first five tend to be those experienced by children who have the inattentive type of ADD without the hyperactive/impulsive component. That is, they display difficulty completing classwork, following directions, getting right down to work, paying attention to the teacher, or trying hard to do assignments. Kids with the hyperactive/impulsive type of ADD not only display many of these first five problem areas, but also have difficulty with numbers six through ten, such as respecting the rights of others (touching and distracting other kids), following class and school rules, talking out of turn or making noises, acting up in special classes, and staying in their seat.

To use this system, ask each teacher to place a blank *DRC* on your child's desk each morning (taping it down will keep it in place and readily visible to both the teacher and the child). The A.M. and P.M. designations distinguish whether the problem occurred before lunch (A.M.) or after lunch (P.M.). Ask the teacher to place a small checkmark in either the A.M. or P.M. column whenever the child is experiencing difficulty in any of the ten problem areas. For example, if your daughter doesn't complete two classwork assignments before lunch, each one is noted with a small checkmark in row number one, A.M. If she gets out of her seat inappropriately (not for acceptable reasons) twice in the morning and three times in the afternoon, there should be two checkmarks in row number ten, A.M., as well as

Figure 10
Daily Report Card (DRC)

Student: _____

Date: _____

Teacher's Signature: _____

Teacher's Signature: _____

✓ = Problem in this area

_____ Total points received

PROBLEM AREAS	A.M.	P.M.	ASSIGNMENTS
1. Completes classwork			Homework and Incomplete Classwork
2. Follows directions			
3. Gets right down to work			
4. Pays attention to teacher			
5. Tries hard to do assignments			"Due" ( ) "None" ( )
6. Respects the rights of others (keeps hands to self, doesn't disturb others)			Projects, Book Reports, Tests, Quizzes Announced
7. Follows class and school rules			
8. Does not talk out of turn. Does not make noises			"Due" ( ) "None" ( )
9. Attitude and behavior is acceptable in special classes (art, music, physical ed., and so on)			Teacher Comments:
10. Stays in seat			

three checkmarks in row number ten, P.M. The checkmarks are placed by the teacher in ink (to deter erasure attempts by the child) as they occur so that your child is always aware of how many checks she's accumulating.

By the end of the school day, or earlier, your daughter should fill in the "Assignments" section of the *DRC* with specific homework and incomplete classwork assignments to be done that night, as well as any projects, book reports, tests, and quizzes announced. The due date is asked for in each of the above cases. Also, there is a "None" box available so that your child can check off if there's no homework assigned or projects announced. The teacher can place a comment, if necessary, in the box provided and then, after checking what *the child* wrote for homework or tests announced, sign the form at the top, which validates its accuracy. There are places for two teachers' signatures and if the child has more than two (such as in middle school) more spaces for teacher signatures can be added. Also, note the spots for the student's name and date on the *DRC* so that you can keep the sheets in chronological order if necessary.

The next part of using the *DRC* system is to incorporate much of the criteria of the *DAS* program, described in my study skills program in Chapter Six. In order to have earned a *Good Day* on the *DRC* program and to receive all of the rewards (I suggest employing the three poker chips, play time/freedom, and electricity for older kids and using treats or trinkets or the red and blue poker chips for kindergarteners or first graders), the child must do *all* of the following:

- Bring home the *DRC* each day, signed by all of the teachers.

- Bring home all materials necessary to complete homework or incomplete classwork, as well as to work on projects, book reports, quizzes, and tests.

- Keep the number of checkmarks at or below the maximum number of checks allowed.

The best way to determine the number of allowable checkmarks to earn a *Good Day* is to have the teacher fill out the "Problem areas" section of the *DRC* for five school days as a baseline experiment, with *no consequences* (either positive or negative) occurring to the child each day. In this manner you'll get a good idea how picky a grader the teacher is, and you'll be able to gauge the average number of checks that your child tends to receive without consequences occurring.

For example, let's say your son received eight checks on Monday of the baseline week and nine, seven, five, and eight Tuesday through Friday, respectively. That averages out to about seven checkmarks per day and he wasn't given consequences for task completion, paying attention, or good behavior. I suggest that he be told that starting the next Monday he'll need to keep the number of checkmarks to six or less each day as his maximum number of checks allowed (one less than his average of seven during the baseline week). If he succeeds and gets six or less checkmarks, as well as bringing home the completed *DRC* with teacher signatures and all necessary homework materials, he then earns a *Good Day* and receives *all* of his rewards. If he doesn't (if he gets seven or more checkmarks, it's not a *Good Day*), then he loses *all* of his daily rewards.

If, after a whole week, you see that at least four of the five days are *Good Days*, pile on the praise and announce that because he's trying so hard and doing so well that you think he's ready to lower the maximum number of allowable checkmarks to five a day beginning the following week. Each week or two continue to lower the allowable number of checks by one, never going below a maximum of two or three checkmarks (many kids, if placed on the *DRC*, will get a couple of checks each day just for acting like kids!)

If this system works well, that is, your son's frequency of acting out, getting out of his seat, not completing classwork, or failing to pay attention to the teacher decreases to an acceptable level, then he probably doesn't have true ADD. (The child with at least moderate to severe ADD can't keep it together all day, every day, in order to lower the checkmarks to three, two, or less.) Your child probably was of the willfully noncompliant variety and changed his classroom behavior and performance due to knowledge of the consequences he'd receive at home later that day. Remember, you must be consistent in checking the *DRC* on a daily basis, as well as the number of checkmarks received and whether all necessary materials are brought home. The most important aspect is that the consequences are given accurately—if your son does not earn a *Good Day* and he still receives his rewards, the *DRC* system will soon become ineffective. If your child responded well to this program and the diagnosis of ADD is ruled out, continue using the *DRC* throughout the school year. It will keep him on track, knowing that you're receiving daily feedback from the teacher and appropriate consequences will be given.

The *DRC* can also be a tremendous help for children with true ADD. The checkmarks continually alert the child throughout the day about how he's doing, and he'll try harder to stay on task. Also, the "Assignment" boxes on the *DRC* teach responsible behavior in terms of writing down teacher expectations, as well as serving as an organizational reminder for packing up the books to bring home at the end of the school day. Since a child with true ADD will probably have a baseline week with an average number of checkmarks higher than the willfully noncompliant child, you may need to start the ADD kid with a maximum allowable number of checkmarks of ten, twelve, or even fourteen per day. Slowly lower the maximum number allowed as the weeks go by and the child learns to become more responsible for his class performance and behavior.

It's not that an ADD child can't pay attention or complete assignments, he just has significantly more difficulty staying on task and remaining motivated to fight the tendency to daydream or to leave his seat. Most kids with ADD do much better in school when using the *DRC*, but many also profit from medication and academic remediation. If all three methods are employed, you'll most likely see the number of checkmarks decreasing significantly (indicating that both the daily consequences and medication are working), as well as more classwork and homework being completed.

Jeremy's Story

Jeremy, age nine, was referred to Dr. Peters by his third grade teacher. Although not a behavior problem, Jeremy's mind would just "drift off" and he would miss assignments from the onset of the day requiring him to engage in hopeless catch-up behavior for the rest of the day. He was miserable about school. Jeremy's home life was very stable and loving. There were no "life issues" distracting him from being a good student. He was certainly bright enough and he'd previously been testing for learning disabilities (none). His struggle was causing simple homework to take most of the evening. Little by little, he lost privileges—his bike, sports, and so on—until he had nothing left and there was still no improvement in his work. By now his attitude toward school was dreadful.

Our mission with Dr. Peters was to answer the question: To medicate for Attention Deficit Disorder or not to medicate? We came to understand that if Jeremy truly needed to be medicated, it would be cruel not to take that route. From the first week of the behavioral approach where Jeremy could earn privileges for better work, he showed immediate improvement in paying attention. His grades improved proportionately. It took just one forty-five-minute time-out session (those pesky consequences) for Jeremy to realize he'd rather be on the earning side of the equation than the paying side. Jeremy had just received a report card with two D's right before he began seeing Dr. Peters. His next report card showed the D's up to B+'s and every other category was improved by one full letter grade.

Jeremy continues to do well with the combination of privileges/allowance incentive combined, with consequences of time-outs. His older sister had him worried about whether he'd even make it to fourth grade. Now he says, "It will be no problem." He is a happy kid again, realizing that paying attention will always be a challenge for him, but he has more control over paying attention than he realized. His life is quite enjoyable and rewarding now. He feels great about just doing well!

Learning Differences

The third main reason that kids have difficulty in school, even when they're giving it their all, is that of a specific learning disability or a learning difference. The latter designation is more preferable, since kids diagnosed as learning disabled, by definition, have average or above intelligence levels and are often quite bright. They're curious and inquisitive and many are very hard workers, although they face frustration daily in the classroom. However, due to what are called cognitive processing deficits, these youngsters have difficulty processing various forms of information that they receive. For example, a child with perfect peripheral hearing (the ear and other parts of the auditory sensory apparatus necessary for adequate auditory input is intact), yet the way that the child's brain *interprets* the auditory sensation (the child's perception and processing of the information) may be inaccurate. If your child is constantly misinterpreting the teacher's oral instructions or lectures, it's difficult to perform adequately in the classroom—it's almost as if she's receiving a different set of class notes than are her classmates!

Processing difficulties are often found to be innate or genetic in nature. Mom or Dad usually have some difficulty in the same area. Also, children who have experienced some sort of brain injury, whether it be prenatal (being exposed to a toxin while in the womb), perinatal (a difficult delivery with decreased oxygen level available at birth), or postnatal (a head injury due to an automobile accident or a severe fall), often exhibit higher than average frequencies of learning problems. The bottom line is that the child with the learning disability, by definition, is of at least average IQ and has adequate sensory sensation capabilities (hearing, vision, and tactile senses are all intact), but the way that the brain is "wired" leads to inaccurate processing of the sensory information received. You can see how difficult it would be to come up with the right answer if your brain interpreted the question differently than it was given.

When discussing learning problems, I prefer to use the term "difference" rather than "disability"—the former has a much less negative connotation and the latter suggests that the child is *unable* to learn and that's far from the truth.

Even kids with severe learning differences can learn, but the teacher has to be creative, finding the best channel to use to present the information accurately.

Learning differences affect the following areas:

- Ability to gather information from the environment (home, school, museum tour, and so on)

- Ability to classify or categorize information (place in order, relate to previously learned material)

- Ability to remember information (phonic rules or math facts)

- Ability to express information (either orally or in written form)

We know that learning occurs best when the information presented comes through the strongest learning channel. The auditory learner gets more out of a class lecture format than reading a textbook, whereas the visual learner succeeds best by seeing a demonstration of the concept. Nancy Boyles and Darlene Contadino in *The Learning Difference Sourcebook* provide an excellent example of the needs of a visual/tactile learner: "A student may hear an explanation about sound waves and see examples in the science book but not fully understand the concept until he touches a tuning fork to water and sees the ripples." These authors further note that research has shown that "Students retain 10 percent of what they read, 26 percent of what they hear, 30 percent of what they see, 50 percent of what they hear and see, 70 percent of what they say, and 90 percent of what they say and do." Obviously having students involved directly (perhaps repeating and teaching the concept) capitalizes on all learning channels and provides for a more successful learning experience.

The assessment of a learning disability or difference, although varying somewhat by the state or school district, generally involves three parts in terms of gathering information about the child:

- An evaluation of the child's ability level (an intelligence test)

- How the youngster's brain collects, organizes, remembers, and expresses information (a cognitive processing battery)

- Strengths and weaknesses in academic areas (achievement testing focusing upon the areas of reading, mathematics, and written language)

Certain criteria have to be met in order for the child to be legally described as having a learning disability and to receive services from a public school system. Although your child may have definite learning differences while failing to meet the school system's criteria by a point or two, he may still benefit from special services. An excellent source of information about assessment of learning disabilities and how placement occurs can be found in Janet Lerner's text, *Learning Disabilities*.

"Teaching to the strengths" tends to be the motto of many learning disability specialists and using the information from the assessment battery described above helps to determine whether your child is a visual, tactile, or auditory learner (none of us learn solely through one channel alone, but most of us do have a preferred channel). For children with learning differences the magnitude of the preference can be great and therefore needs to be employed in the child's individualized educational plan.

Visual learners often benefit from learning how to create a mental picture of what's being taught or using graphs, maps, diagrams, or actual demonstrations. These kids tend to be better sight-word readers than phonetic readers. Auditory learners benefit from a "books on tape" format so that the knowledge gained from reading the text is reinforced later by listening to it again on audio tape. They're usually better phonetic readers than sight-word readers. Tactile learners tend to get a lot of information from hands-on experiences, such as using blocks to teach mathematics concepts, viewing demonstrations, as well as engaging in laboratory experiments.

So if your child is displaying a significant learning difference, conference with your school guidance counselor as well as the teacher. If, upon assessment, it is determined that she meets criteria for special services at her school, take a look at what's being offered. Interview the learning specialist to see if the program will be individualized enough to meet your child's needs. If not, or your daughter doesn't meet criteria for admission into a special program, consider a private learning center or a special learning tutor for help in bolstering her weak areas. Remember, teach to her strengths—if she's an auditory learner use the "books on tape" approach (information your school's administrator will be able to provide), but also insist that she read the text, even though you're backing it up with knowledge presentation on audio tape upon completion of reading.

Using my study skills program is also very helpful for kids displaying learning differences. Often these children are so frustrated during the school day that they purposefully avoid writing down assignments and test dates because studying can be so draining, or they've actually missed the teacher's announcement of the assignments, especially if your kid is a visual learner and the assignment was presented orally and not written on the blackboard. Following the plan will help keep your child on task and prepared for tomorrow's lessons. She'll feel more secure knowing that she can answer questions if called upon and may even venture to volunteer in class. This helps with her self-esteem, an area that's notoriously shaky for children with learning differences.

eight

Giving the Gift

~~~~~

As we've seen, academic achievement is more a product of appropriate placement of priorities and responsible behavior than it is of intelligence. There are lots of bright kids who flunk classes, brilliant high schoolers who drop out and quick-witted adults who can't seem to hold a job or effectively face challenges at home or in the workplace. Almost any child can do well at school whether they have low, average, or superior ability. What seems to count the most is one's work ethic and willingness to tolerate frustration—to continue to tackle tough math problems, even though your first impulse is to give up, and to bring home and study the science text, even though tonight is the season finale of a favorite television sitcom.

This type of prioritizing is often not innate—it's learned by watching others (generally parents), receiving guidance and supervision (by Mom and Dad), as well as by making the connection between behavior and consequences (yep, performed by Mom and Dad again!).

There's no escaping the role that parental involvement plays in your child's academic career. Remember what Secretary of Education, Lauro Cavasos found after reviewing hundreds of studies focusing on academic achievement? That *the single best predictor of academic success is parental involvement.* That's not only a stunning statement but a heavy obligation. *Leave it to the teacher* parents, those doing the *denial dance,* and *peace at any price* folks have a difficult time rising to the occasion. Many kids are just not mature enough to see the value of education and they need a jump-start from you, the parent, to help them to internalize the work ethic. My study skills program serves as the best organizational system, as well as external motivating source that I'm aware of, and this plan will be one of the best gifts that you can ever give to your child.

The Bases of Self-Concept

Not only does academic achievement lead to so many varied opportunities in life, but it also helps tremendously with self-esteem. Your child's self-concept is based upon how she feels about and compares herself with her peers in the following areas:

➤ **Academic**—"Am I smart?", "Will I give a stupid answer in class and the kids make fun of me?", "Do others value my ideas?"

➤ **Physical**—"Am I pretty?", "Do I have a good body?", "Am I attractive to others?"

➤ **Social**—"Do kids want to play with me?", "Does the telephone ring or am I doing most of the phone calling?", "Do I have someone to eat lunch with each day?"

➤ **Athletic**—"Am I picked near the top when teams are chosen?", "Can I hold my own on the ball field?", "Am I strong?"

Having been a child myself, raised two of them, and worked with thousands of children in my therapy practice, I've come to the conclusion that the key to solid self-esteem lies in feeling good about oneself in at least one of these areas. And, it's important to note that it's not how others see the child, but how *the kid feels others perceive her.*

If your daughter is complaining about her freckles, the size of her feet, or shape of her nose, no amount of parental soothing ("You're being overcritical, all the girls in our family have solid, size twelve feet") will make a dent in the kid's self-perception. She has to feel it in her own heart in order to believe it. The bases of kid self-concept—their self-perceptions of academic ability, physical attractiveness, social popularity, and athletic prowess are what matter. *They need to feel significant*—that they are special in at least one area, and that others notice and value them for this.

You may note that some very important character traits, such as honesty, helpfulness, compassion, and caring, are missing from this list. It's a shame, though, but these characteristics are often not valued until later years when the child enters the adult world and playground politics are no longer as important. I've come to believe that this is the reason why navigating adolescence successfully is so difficult to accomplish. As young children and preteens, it's easier to fit in—others are more accepting and less critical, you can miss a hoop shot and still be liked, lots of kids wear braces on their teeth, and parents can still pick friends for their children and help cement relationships. Being friendly and compassionate is noticed and goes a long way toward being accepted by peers.

However, it's a whole different ball game at the middle- and high school levels—a few bad hair days can cause huge embarrassment, not catching the subtleties of a joke leads to being teased, and claiming the "wrong" music group is a ticket to ostracism. Being seen as caring, compassionate, a good friend, or using good judgment do not necessarily lead to popularity points. More emphasis is placed upon whether the kid wears the right clothes, sits with the correct group at lunch, makes the cheerleading squad, or answers correctly in class.

As adults, the cycle continues to evolve. Not only do physical attractiveness, social skills, and athletic prowess continue to be important to our adult self-concept, but we tend to increase the value placed upon academic success—be it knowledge for a rousing game of Trivial Pursuit, answering before the actual players do when watching

Jeopardy on television, graduating from college, or landing a great job due to computer skills or an excellent college grade-point average. In addition, traits such as caring, compassion, and persistence play an even greater role as we look to find committed, long-lasting personal relationships with people whom we can trust for the long haul.

This book is about academic success. Of all the bases of self-concept described above, this area is the one most within your child's control and your influence. Appropriate study skills guarantee good grades and excellent performance. Study skills are merely actions, and self-esteem is based on esteemable acts. It follows, therefore, that the greater the quantity and quality of study actions your child performs, the greater the number of esteemable acts will be attributed to her. The larger the number of esteemable acts, the more solid and stable will be her self-concept. The connection between parents motivating kids to employ good study skills and the resulting self-esteem level is strong.

You have somewhat less influence and your child has somewhat less control in terms of her physical attractiveness. You've already contributed your DNA, and for better or worse, she's walking around with either her mother's or father's hair color, shape of nose, propensity for weight gain and height. Modifications to physical attractiveness can be made to some extent, including contributing money to purchase the right clothes, a neat haircut, braces for crooked teeth, contacts instead of glasses, and in some cases, even a nose job.

As your kid matures, you'll have even less control as a parent when it comes to your child's social popularity.

With little kids parents can have a large impact by becoming the neighborhood "Cookie Mom"—kids will play with your children if for no better reason than the smell of chocolate chips baking in the oven. Once they're over, though, your child has to kick in with interesting things to do, new games to play, or a facility for Nintendo. As kids mature, cookies become less important and the burden of learning to successfully work a crowd falls more upon the child. Hopefully she's learned some social skills—good eye contact, telling a joke or two, and is not afraid to take social risks and to speak out in groups.

The fourth basis for self-concept is that of athletics, which is partially influenced by DNA (predetermined height, body structure, musculature), as well as the environmental stimulation that parents can provide. Most kids become proficient at a sport due to practice, practice, and more practice. Odds are that the boy with his own basketball hoop will try more layup shots than does a child who has to ride his bike to get to the hoop at the gym. Involvement on baseball, soccer, gymnastics, and swim teams provide the repetitions necessary for success, and usually perseverance pays off. Your daughter may not make it to the Olympics, but gymnastic lessons during grade school will help set her up for selection to the cheerleading squad later when she's in high school.

Setting the Scene for
Good Self-Esteem

In the large scheme of things I believe that academic achievement is the most important basis for good self-esteem. Remember the cycle of self-concept, how kids' values change over time? To little ones, appearing smart (knowing the answers when called upon, being able to name all seven continents, not asking silly questions in class) is paramount. Prepared pre- and grade-schoolers are attractive to others—they're seen as not only interesting, but fun to be with. They have good ideas for new ways to use a jump rope in various games, come up with interesting group science projects, and are great to call at night for help on the math worksheet. Feeling smart in this stage of life is terrific—others look up to you, teachers call upon you, and your folks actually claim you!

As high school approaches and arrives, the other three bases (physical attractiveness, socialization skills, and athletic prowess) become more significant, but the youngster needs to strike a balance between the four areas. It's not fun being a good student if no one will sit with you at lunch, and weekends tend to be boring without a friend to play with or a ball game to go to. Making good grades and being respected academically is not a guarantee to fitting in socially. It does serve, though, as a terrific foundation for the adolescent balancing act when looking attractive, wearing the correct clothes, making a high school sports team, and working the lunch crowd successfully are all important attributes.

Academic achievers are also seen as school leaders. In grade school they get picked more often to clean the blackboard, to mentor younger kids, and are trusted by teachers to take notes to the office. In middle and high school they often hold positions in student government organizations and are chosen to receive awards and college scholarships. These kids are known—they are *significant, important*, and *special*—keys to feeling good about oneself. Not everyone can be an athlete, have great looks, or socialize in an uninhibited manner. Many kids have to deal with being overweight, clumsy, or painfully shy. But they can have great grades and feel smart if they have followed my study skills program and have developed the skills, habits, and perseverance necessary for good academic achievement. Remember, the difference between an A student and a C student is often not based in intelligence, it's a matter of sweat equity—how much one is willing to put into studying and completing tasks.

And the cycle of self-concept continues as we mature. Often I see a shift of what is important as kids graduate high school, attend college, or start a vocation, get married, and have children of their own. Sure, looking like Julia Roberts or Brad Pitt doesn't hurt and social extroverts tend to have an easier go at it than do the painfully shy, but what really comes to the fore is the work ethic developed in the earlier academic settings. Employers look for grade-point averages when they hire, and responsibility behaviors and productivity when they promote. Prospective spouses, often initially attracted by physical appearance, remain impressed by earning capacity, responsibility, commitment, and stability (often outcomes of learning good frustration tolerance as a kid). Marriages continue not because Dad can shoot hoops well, but because he provides for the family by finding and keeping a good job and acting in a loving and responsible manner. Mom remains attractive to Dad not only because she works out or looks great in a bathing suit, but because she's up on the daily news, has interests, and therefore is interesting, and is fulfilled in her career at the workplace or does a good job keeping the house and kids on track. All of these attributes are based in maturity, self-discipline, and good frustration tolerance—the very aspects that your child learns when doing homework that he isn't necessarily interested in, but completes because of his good work ethic.

Parents contribute to their child's academic success both through donating DNA (kid IQs are consistently found to be highly related to their parents' intellectual abilities), as well as to environmental factors. In fact, the latter is often more important than genetics. I'll take a motivated kid with an average IQ any day over a brilliant child who is an unmotivated slug. The first type completes their work, figures out the value of education, and tends to become more successful later in life than their brilliant but lazy counterparts who never quite seem to work to their predicted potential. It's easy to start projects, but it's those who can persevere and finish them who are most valued by society.

So if you want to help your kid with her self-concept, there are many things you can do. Save up for the braces and figure out how she can have some nice outfits to wear.

Shoot hoops and throw the football with your son. Talk to your children about social skills, such as good eye contact, smiling at others, telling jokes, and becoming a good listener. But most of all—set the stage for them to feel smart. Teach good study skills and habits, expect classwork and homework to be completed on a daily basis. Talk about going to college as a strong possibility. Show up at school functions and become as involved as you can. Value education and show it yourself in your daily life. Help your kids to keep a balance in their lives—using strengths as a basis for solid self-concept, and shoring up weaknesses so that they fit in well with others. Guide them, for if you don't, they may flounder trying to figure out the rules of the road, or worse yet—depend upon their peers' experience and wisdom for guidance (now, that's a scary thought!).

Remember, your child needs to perceive himself as significant and important in order to feel good about himself, now as well as in his later years. Many parents have confided to me how unfilled they now feel because they didn't step out there as kids, working harder, taking social risks, or planning ahead. They're now reaping the negatives of the poor seeds that they sowed at an early age, and are unhappy, bitter, or resentful at forty-five. You can help your child to avoid this all-too-familiar scenario by encouraging her as a child to persist when frustrated, to take her schoolwork seriously, and to form a solid basis for today's as well as tomorrow's self-concept and success.

This type of dedication requires your time, patience, and most of all, love. It's easy to put the responsibility on others or to give up and take a sink-or-swim attitude when your child slacks off in school. It takes character to develop and to implement my study skills program—there will be days when you wish that your child would see the light and finally "get it," valuing his education, becoming internally motivated to complete homework and to study for tests. That day will come if you give him the gift of organization and study skills provided by my program. And the bonus of a good self-concept is hard to beat! So step up to the plate and be a hitter—use the techniques that I've given to you and watch your kids' grades improve and family relationships soar. I guarantee that it will be the best gift that you'll ever have the honor of bestowing upon your children!

References and
Suggested Reading

~~~~~~

Albert, Linda. *Coping with Kids*. New York: Ballantine Books, 1984.

Albert, Linda. *A Teacher's Guide to Cooperative Discipline*. Circle Pines Minn.: American Guidance Service, 1989.

American Psychiatric Association. *Diagnostic and Statistical Manual of Mental Disorders*, Fourth ed. Washington, D.C.: American Psychiatric Association, 1994.

Arnold, Karen D. *Lives of Promise: What Becomes of High School Valedictorians*. San Francisco: Josey-Bass, 1995.

Barkley, Russell A. *Attention Deficit Hyperactivity Disorder: A Handbook for Diagnosis and Treatment*. New York: Guilford Press, 1990.

Boyles, Nancy S., and Darlene Contadino. *The Learning Differences Sourcebook*. Lincolnwood, Ill.: NTC/Contemporary Publishing Group, 1998.

Brazelton, T. Berry. *Touchpoints: Your Child's Emotional and Behavioral Development*. Reading, Mass.: Addison-Wesley, 1992.

Canter, Lee. *Homework Without Tears for Teachers*. Santa Monica, Calif.: Lee Canter and Associates, 1988.

_____. and Lee Hausner. *Homework Without Tears*. New York: Harper & Row, 1987.

Ch.A.D.D. Education Committee, *Attention Deficit Disorders: A Guide for Teachers*. Plantation, Fla.: Ch.A.D.D., 1988.

Clark, Lynn. *The Time-out Solution: A Parent's Guide for Handling Everyday Behavior Problems*. Chicago: Contemporary Books, 1989.

Conners, C. Keith, and Karen C. Wells. *Hyperkinetic Children*. Beverly Hills, Calif.: Sage Publications, 1986.

Dobson, James. *The New Dare to Discipline*. New York: Tyndale House, 1992.

Dodson, Fitzhugh. *How to Discipline with Love: From Crib to College*. New York: New American Library, 1978.

Elkind, David. *The Hurried Child*. Reading, Mass.: Addison–Wesley, 1982.

_____. *Ties That Stress*. Cambridge, Mass. Harvard University Press, 1994.

Faber, Adele, and Elaine Mazlish. *Siblings Without Rivalry: How to Help Your Children Live Together So You Can Live Too*. New York: Norton, 1987.

_____. *How to Talk So Kids Will Listen and Listen So Kids Will Talk*. New York: Avon Books, 1980.

Friedman, Ronald J., and Guy T. Doyal. *Attention Deficit Disorder and Hyperactivity*. Second ed. Danville, Ill.: The Interstate Publishing, 1987.

Fry, Ron. *How to Study*. Franklin Lakes, N.J.: Career Press, 1996.

Goleman, Daniel. *Emotional Intelligence*. New York: Bantam Books, 1995.

Greenspan, Stanley I., and Beryl Lieff Benderly. *The Growth of the Mind*. Reading, Mass.: Perseus Books, 1997.

Gross, David A., and Irl L. Extein. *A Parent's Guide to Common and Uncommon School Problems*. Washington, D.C.: PIA Press, 1989.

Harper, Timothy. *Labeled—but Disabled? Sky* magazine (Sept. 1996): 87–93.

Ingersoll, Barbara. *Your Hyperactive Child: A Parent's Guide to Coping with Attention Deficit Disorder*. New York: Doubleday, 1988.

Kagan, Jerome. *The Nature of the Child*. New York: Basic Books, 1984.

Lavin, Paul. *Parenting the Overactive Child: Alternatives to Drug Therapy*. Lanham, Md.: Madison Books, 1989.

Lerner, Janet. *Learning Disabilities*. Boston: Houghton Mifflin, 1988.

Peck, M. Scott. *The Road Less Traveled: A New Psychology of Love, Traditional Values, and Spiritual Growth*. New York: Touchstone, 1978.

Peters, Ruth A. *Don't Be Afraid to Discipline*. New York: Golden Books, 1997.

_____. *It's Never Too Soon to Discipline*. New York: St. Martin's Press, 1999.

Pipher, Mary. *Reviving Ophelia: Saving the Souls of Adolescent Girls*. New York: Ballantine Books, 1994.

Poretta, Vicki, and Marian Edelman Borden. *Mom's Guide to Raising a Good Student*. New York: Alpha Books, 1997.

Rimm, Sylvia. *Dr. Sylvia Rimm's Smart Parenting*. New York: Crown Publishing Group, 1996.

Rosemond, John. *Parent Power: A Common-Sense Approach to Parenting in the 90's and Beyond*. Kansas City: Andrews & McMeel, 1990.

Rosemond, John. *Ending the Homework Hassle*. New York: Andrews & McMeel, 1990.

Silverman, Marvin, and David Lustig. *Parent Survival Training*. North Hollywood, Calif.: Wilshire Book Company, 1987.

Weiss, Gabrielle, and Lily Trokenberg-Hechtman. *Hyperactive Children Grown Up*. New York: Guilford Press, 1986.

Wender, Paul H. *The Hyperactive Child. Adolescent, and Adult: Attention Deficit Disorder Through the Lifespan*. New York: Oxford University Press, 1987.

Zametkin, A. J., et al. "Cerebral Glucose Metabolism in Adults with Hyperactivity of Childhood Onset." *New England Journal of Medicine*. 323 (20), 1990: 1361–66.

Ziglar, Zig. *Raising Positive Kids in a Negative World*. New York: Ballantine Books, 1989.